Best wishes

Wilderland

Wildlife and Wonder from the Shropshire Borders Andrew Fusek Peters

previous pages **Rescue orphan badger** *Meles meles* **at Cuan Wildlife Rescue:** Canon 1dx, 100mm macro, 1/400 sec, F2.8, ISO 1250
Lesser Redpoll *Carduelis cabaret*: Canon 1dx, 500mm + 1.4x, 1/200 sec, F10, ISO 400, 3 Yongnuo flashes **Peregrine falcon** *Falco peregrinus*: Canon 7d2, 500mm + 1.4x, 1/320 sec, F8, ISO 500

Bog pool on the Long Mynd at dawn
Canon 6d, 16-35mm, 2.5 sec, F13, ISO 50, grad filters, tripod, remote release cable
Sunset, Mears Barn: Canon 1dx, 16-35mm, 1/50 sec, F8, ISO 500, grad filters

Wilderland

Wildlife and Wonder from the Shropshire Borders Andrew Fusek Peters

Border Song

All I am is eye and lid,
    A prayer now for what is hid.
All I do is shutter song,
    Flick of feather in a throng.
All I think is softly good,
    Barking in an antlered wood.
All I see is vale and hill,
    The lowing sun, the rising trill.
All I hear is dawn of day,
    The hunt for light and moony prey.
All I cry for those so cold,
    Who crush the wild for foolish gold.
All I feel with heart in hand,
    This my love for this my land.

Andrew Fusek Peters photo: Geoff Ward

First published in Great Britain in 2016 by Fair Acre Press

www.fairacrepress.co.uk

Copyright © Andrew Fusek Peters *(pictures and text)*

Graphic design: Tim Keates

Set in 10/14pt Plantin

A catalogue record for this book is available from the British Library

Printed by Latitude Press Limited

ISBN 978-1-911048-03-9

If I had not been editing the Wenlock Poetry Festival anthology of 2014 I would not have read Andrew Fusek Peters' poem *Blackbird*, noticed it was one line longer than my printing stipulations, asked the printers to squeeze another millimetre onto the book's height to accommodate it, remembered his name…

I have read a lot of poems on the subject of blackbirds but for me his captures, like none other, that gentle learning of another species through our daily coexistence: On winter afternoons, like many I'm sure, I put away my garden fork once I hear the blackbird sing.

If Anna Dreda and I had not been running an anthology tour that same year I may not have met Andrew – and Anna would not have made the suggestion, in the George and Dragon, Much Wenlock, that we might want to work together.

If I had not had the idea of publishing a book of poetry and art on the butterflies of Shropshire – found willing and talented contributors; discovered how a good layout of a book makes me feel alive; created a finely bound limited edition book Three Poets on William Penny Brookes, a Much Wenlock Man; published wonderful poets from Shropshire; or found myself drawn back to projects about the history of the Universe, about Maligned Species – then I would not have been open to Anna's idea.

If Andrew's family, and Tim's family had not been out walking the Stiperstones at the exact same moment in time and space: they might never have met, laughed together, found common ground.

This book has surpassed all my hopes – I am so proud to be publishing it. I have gasped when proof reading the drafts, and am humbled by the joy and love within these pages.

Thank you Andrew and Tim, thank you.

Thank you to all the people who work to keep our countryside, and to all of you who recognise its beauty, its fascinations, its truths.

Nadia Kingsley **www.fairacrepress.co.uk**

'How charming it would be if it were possible to cause these natural images to imprint themselves durable and remain fixed upon the paper. And why should it not be possible? I asked myself'

William Henry Fox Talbot

I have lived in Shropshire my whole married life, but only picked up a camera four years ago. The borders have been my swimming hole, my walking adventure, my children's playground. For twenty five years, I have marvelled at the folding bulk of the Long Mynd, the sudden rearing of roe deer from the wood at Linley, the far darting blue of kingfisher and the midnight boogy-shuffle of badger. Yet these sights were only of passing interest, the background to the landscape of my living days and nights. I had family, work and a whole soupçon of delightful and exhausting distractions from what lay in front of my eyes.

The camera changed everything. This impossible object in my hands, with its evolutionary complications, was a species in its own right that could easily bear a lifetime's study. When I lifted it to my eye and sharpened my focus, the Marches were remade into new and surprising territory. How could I know that barn owl, when hungry, sometimes hunted by day? Or that wren, in a display of tiny insouciance, would build his nest in the hedge where I park my car? This was a third eye, which when opened, revealed Eden, or at the very least a wildlife that struggled to persist alongside humanity. Each October, our county transformed to a facsimile of Canada as huge salmon leaped the weir at Ludlow and Shrewsbury. When my friend Ric told me about this, I laughed in disbelief at such local magnificence. Only the sight of silver, waterborne beings taking to the air through a flick of muscle, was I convinced and then, utterly blown away. Slowly, through diligence, and stalking, and hours, and days, and friends, and persistence, I discovered a different OS map that lay beneath the footpath friendly way.

This map was not only concerned with place, but time, hour and season. If those figures matched up and coincided, then there was the possibility of: crossbills in November at Bury Ditches; bitterns in February at Welshpool; linnets, summer dawns and purple heather under a full moon on the Stiperstones; ravens cruising all year round the airways and airport rocks of the Long Mynd.

The list goes on, added to only by experience, walking, looking, listening. We call Shropshire the borderlands, and my borders began to expand every day.

Even landscape became a target to stalk. It had a territory – the top of the Stiperstones, the Long Mynd, Bury Ditches and a time when best to see it display all its landed glory – the quiet moments when the world sleeps or is elsewhere about the busy-ness of life. Dawn, dusk and the starlit night were the aim of my lens, camera body and settings. The capture of light, be it rising, falling or spread across the sky in an infinite seasoning of bright and hot pepper.

Here is a flavour then of what I have found: stories of wildlife rescue, farmers fighting to save new born lambs, the great grace of hawk flight and the flare of first fledglings from peregrine to flycatcher, the dance of hare and stare of fox, the mist that coddles all of dawn on Christmas Eve, the Milky Way that splays its disco lights above the Stiperstones. This could be called a love song, or a summing up of all that I hold dear about my county. I hope it is not a requiem, found in a dusty box in some hundred years where children marvel at the animals and birds long gone. Maybe, if enough beauty is reflected back from lens, and paper and pages of a book, it might make us pause to think and hopefully fight to save this sliver of wilderness from the inexorable hand of progress.

Female Roe deer *Capreolus capreolus* **Lydbury North:** Canon 7d, 150-600,
1/1000 sec, F6.3, ISO 2500 **Kingfisher** *Alcedo atthis* **with Three-spined
stickleback** *Gasterosteus aculeatus*: Canon 1dx, 500mm, 1/500 sec, F4, ISO 400
Walcot Lake at dawn: Canon 6d, 17-40mm, 1/500 sec, F4, ISO 100

Acknowledgements

I want to thank my publisher Nadia Kingsley, who had faith in the project from the start, and Anna Dreda, the supportive friend who introduced us. Along the way, Ben Osborne has been a great mate and mentor, and Alan Ward a good photo buddy. I have learnt so much about photography and many Shropshire sites from the wonderful friendship of Ric Morris. A big thank you to Pete Carty of the National Trust who has been behind my pics all the way, and to Simon Cooter of Natural England both for his commissioning me with Pete to do the *Stepping Stones* project but also for a series of amazing Stiperstones dawn excursions. I am grateful to Alan Reid for taking me in during the deer rut. Anna, Sean, Fran, Pam, Megan, Claire and the team opened the doors of Cuan House Wildlife Rescue and made me so welcome. I am also grateful for the support of Shropshire Wildlife Trust as I have developed my photography. Much of the book could not have happened without helpful and informative farmers and landowners, including Steve & Ruth at Mears Barn, Jonathan Leeke, Tim Ashton, Janet & Jeremy, Derek & Eileen, Philipa, Lynne Wright, Mr & Mrs Cookson and Jim Gafney. I do apologise if I have left anybody out. The design and layout of this book is entirely due to Tim Keates, whose incredibly hard work and visual flare show him to be a graphic-design genius.

Above all, a massive debt to my wife Polly for backing me in this new career, balancing out my mad mood swings and helping me to keep it real and remember the spirit behind this new adventure. And a final acknowledgement to my lovely mum, without whom I might not have been able to do this in the first place.

Sunset from Stiperstones panorama: 6 stitched photos, Canon 6d, 100-400mm, 1/40 sec, F8, ISO 500 **Full moon with red kite flying past, Mears Barn:** Canon 1dx, 500mm, 1/250 sec, F5.6 ISO 1000

Photo acknowledgements

	page
Barn owl hunting published on the cover of Shropshire Wildlife Trust Magazine	18
Tawny owl chick shortlisted Amateur Photographer of the Year 2015	43
Hare in the snow published Shropshire Wildlife Trust Magazine	10
Cuan House Wildlife Rescue photos shortlisted BWPA 2015	16-19
A selection of the Cuan House Wildlife Rescue shots are published as greetings cards by Cuan Wildlife Rescue	
Hare, Mears Barn published Shropshire Wildlife Trust Magazine	46-47
Bridgnorth Otters published, What's What Magazine	56-59
Blackbird mother in shed shortlisted BWPA 2014	65
Kingfisher photos published What's What Magazine	83-85
Hare close up portrait published on cover of The Hare Book (Graffeg), in The Hare Preservation Trust Calender 2015 and on the cover, Hare Preservation Trust Calendar 2016	96

	page
Full moon over Devil's Chair, Stiperstones published in The Guardian	117
Dog Otter, English Bridge published Shropshire Wildlife Trust Magazine	128-129
Displaying Pheasant, Mears Barn published in The Times and on The Guardian website	131
Male and female brown hare boxing published on The Guardian website	152

A selection of the wildlife photos are published by Chris George Cards
http://www.chrisgeorgecards.com/categories/wildlife-photography

This book is dedicated to Ric Morris. 'Massive thanks to Ben Osborne – mate, mentor and incredible supporter.'

Winter

Winter in Shropshire is a season of contrasts. On the dull days, when the light is low, the Long Mynd, rearing its bulk high above the Shrewsbury plain, feels like a slouching beast, darkly dragging us into endless long nights. I don't mind afternoons and mornings like this, for this is the weather we have. But when the clouds clear off, then these shorter days produce a clarity in the sky that is breathtaking. Our red kite, so rare twenty five years ago, now soars above everyday fields revealing a great hawk feather-finery. When buzzard comes down for my road kill pheasant, the corn stubble sings in the December sun. After a storm, the same field above my house shows a rainbow to the west. A buzzard flies through all that vibrancy, unaware it has become the reference point for a blessed view.

When the rain is too constant, I have two indoor projects to keep me busy: firstly, I have been honoured to photograph the dedicated work at Cuan Wildlife Rescue. From swans that have flown into pylons to orphan badgers and stroppy barn owls, I've been witness to their expertise and compassion; secondly, the feeders in my garden, placed strategically on pretty looking branches, have provided hours of birding delight. Standing in my kitchen with my lens trained through double glazing while I sip a decent cup of assam is not the worst wildlife assignment I have ever been on. There is a magnificence in the common: a woodpecker's flared wing, the snowy fight of goldfinches captured mid action and the wood mouse caught with its own reflection.

On Christmas Eve, I rise early, sensing the promise of day; determined to catch it on the Stiperstones. I drive, then climb the tricky paths in an anticipation that soon rewards me. The glow that seeps into rock and wind-beaten heather belies a warmth that spreads through my body. Here is the gift of Christmas: being present and well wrapped up.

Long Mynd at dusk: Canon 6d, 16-35mm, 1/40 sec, F8, ISO 3200, Lee grad filters **Brown hare** *Lepus europaeus* **in the snow, Lydbury North:** Canon 1dx, 500mm + 1.4x, 1/1000 sec, F8, ISO 125 **Soaring kite** *Milvus milvus*, **Lydham:** Canon 7d, 400mm, 1/800 sec, F6.3, ISO 200

January brings its own gifts with sharp snowfalls dusting the hills. It is almost an act of faith to find the snow that is only a raining dream down in Lydbury North. Even more elusive is the bittern that comes to spend time at Coed y Dinas, where patience is required right into the dusk until this rare bird rises through the reeds.

There is one last, late blast of the Siberian visitor, bringing a further heap of snow to pile around the valleys. It's cold enough to bring out barn owl by day, hunting right in front of lucky me, who has a camera to hand. Winter, like the snow, finally melts away and the hares, who have no burrows to hide in through all that cold weather, are out and about. With hard-worked fieldcraft, where standing still for long enough just about turns me into a tree, hare runs right towards me, so close I find it hard to fit this furred acceleration into my lens. All is well, and spring is coming at last.

All at Mears Barn: hide at dawn: Canon 6d, 16-35mm, 1/40 sec, F8, ISO 1000 **Buzzard portrait:** Canon 1dx, 500mm + 1.4x 1/2000 sec, F7.1, ISO 500 **Staring Buzzard** *Buteo buteo* **and Buzzard with feather in beak:** Canon 1dx, 500mm + 1.4x 1/1250 sec, F6.3, ISO 640 **Buzzard taking off:** Canon 6d, 500mm + 1.4x, 1/1000 sec, F5.6, ISO 1600

I would love to bring the mighty buzzard closer to hand. However, these raptors always know when I slow my car to spy them in a tree or on a post. Generally, before I have even feathered my brakes, they have lifted themselves into the sky with an easy disinterest. So, I must play the big game. My friend Rob knocks me up a miniature, flat-pack house. It has doors, unfolding windows and a roof. The result, painted dark green sits well in the hedge line of Steve's farm. I have a window of six weeks before he ploughs the field. This high view of distant Heath Mynd and Linley Hill is all mine. There are plenty of roadkill pheasants around to set my photo trap and this is the deal. I will feed this most magnificent of hawks, but out of that, I expect a portrait or two. What I had not bargained for was days of snow and howling winter wind that scrapes the field and throws the chill into my face, nor the numbness of sitting for hours in an uninsulated shack while nothing much happens. Over 18 days, I get two cautious visits. Buzzard is hungry but I am the one feasting on the view. Recent studies have shown that people kill far more pheasants, through shooting and car incidents, than birds of prey and that buzzards can actually help with pheasant numbers by killing other predators of pheasant eggs and chicks. We have seen too many poisonings of our hawks round here, mainly by gamekeepers and pigeon fanciers. Our great birds need to be supported rather than sacrificed.

Mitchells Fold stone circle at sunset: Canon 6d, 16-35mm, 1/100 sec, F10, ISO 100, grad filters, tripod
The Wrekin and Stretton Hills from Long Mynd before dawn: Canon 6d, 16-35mm, 1/8 sec, F8, ISO 200, tripod, remote release

I have recently met Sean, Anna, Fran and the very committed team who run Cuan Wildlife Rescue. Over 2,000 animals were brought in last year from all over Shropshire. Today we are looking at an injured buzzard. Fran tells me it's been hit by a truck on a roundabout in Telford. I love my car, but its convenience means there is consequence to our speedy evolution.

People under-rate buzzards as if the lack of being a golden eagle is a serious Shropshire self-worth issue. However, they are magnificent, peaty-brown bundles of aerial energy. There is a sad tenderness in the way Fran expertly probes the injury. The news is literally crushing. A smashed pelvis means it will not be able to fend for itself again. It is going to be PTS – Put To Sleep. This is the ethos of Cuan. If an animal can recover, it will be helped back into the wild. If not, it would be cruel to keep such wildness in a cage. I am a witness to a bright-eyed life fading into death. I hope my pictures give both staff and bird some dignity and make us pause to think as we hit that throttle along our county lanes.

Buzzard head portrait: Canon 1dx, 100mm macro, 1/80 sec, F10, ISO 16000 **Fran's hands:** Canon 1dx, 100mm macro, 1/250 sec, F10, ISO 400, flash **Dead buzzard being held:** Canon 1dx, 100mm macro, 1/50 sec, F4, ISO 1000

PTS

There are no wolves here any more,
    the Lion of England is gone.
What growls instead is a dream of
    thought made metal,
horse and cart snapped up in a wink.
    We shake our fists at storms.
Corners cower in terror
    as we chase down speed like prey.

Magnificent buzzard, she of the peat-bog wing,
    hung upon the air
deigning to lower herself to a land of folded vale,
    dine in that dainty way, where she will
even suck on the quill of a feather…
    until that sudden slap…

This skittering eye is shrinking into the night.
    The driver does not pause to finish what's begun,
but slinks away like the beast to Bethlehem,
    where violence is a side-effect of A to 'fucking get
    out of my way' Z.

A stranger comes
    all soul for the sorrow she sees on the road.
Buzzard is hooded by an old rag to give her dark;
    the hawk trick to calm her,
carried here, to Fran, years of tender knowledge
    in the probing fingers.
The broken femur is confirmed
    and with it, the never return to the wild.

Oh the face of Fran as buzzard,
    is wiped out by all that we hold truly economic.
The eye closes slowly as the drug takes,
    revealing in its lid, a webbed silk of white
for even in death
    nature outpaces all our machinations
and we trail behind, bent at the border.

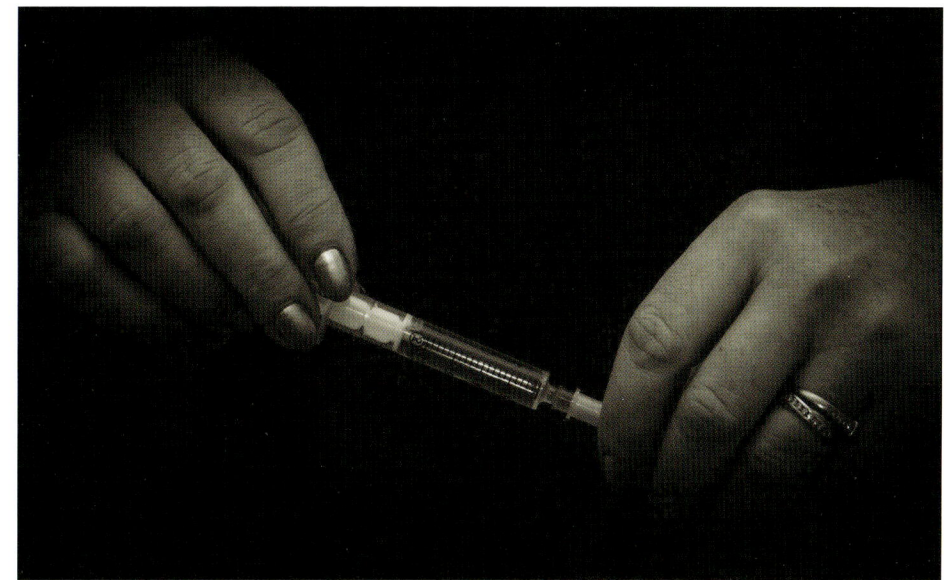

Common pipistrelle bat *Pipistrellus pipistrellus* **being fed:** Canon 1dx,
100mm macro, 1/200 sec, F13, ISO 400, flash **Tawny owl** *Strix aluco* **chick in**
Fran's hands: Canon 1dx, 100mm macro, 1/200 sec, F2.8, ISO 800
Barn owl *Tyto alba***:** Canon 1dx, 100mm macro, 1/200 sec, F10, ISO 160, flash
Barn owl being released: Canon 1dx, 70-200mm, 1/1000 sec, F2.8, ISO 2500

There are many success stories at Cuan. When I see the pipistrelle bat, found rather too awake in Coalport museum when it should be hibernating, how can I not feel wonder? The tininess, the perfection, its little mouth sucking on the greasy innards of a mealworm mixed with Lectade, the animal equivalent of Lucozade. The barn owl, found in a poor state by the side of a road near Bishops Castle, has made a marvellous recovery and we are able at dusk to release it in a friend's field nearby, a stand-out whiteness fading into night. This wonderful charity, always in need of funds and donations, has my support.

Blackbird

Snow has come and swallowed sound,
    Layering the frozen ground.
Steps that clanged now muffled in
    The opposite of daylight's din.

Blackbird sings out loud despite
    The gradual dawning of the night.
Winter will not find redress
    Against this jaunty stubbornness.

Through fading fog, the last few geese,
    Aim for where the land must cease.
Safety is their instinct's ache
    For low, bright water of the lake.

Before the dark shall shut its door
    Hear the perching semaphore.
Blackbird sings and flings his song
    And kin through throat, his echoes throng.

Dusk now wears a paper crown
    Golden lit, the gilded town.
Shadow shall the trees submerge.
    Sett and den and perch, the urge.

To fold in wing, to dream and brood,
    To curl around the season's mood.
Hedge for home, he's tucked in tight
    Blackbird, breathing, silent, night.

My friend owns a few acres of woodland near Bishops Castle, where the badgers are generally safe from lampers and from the tiny minority of farmers that have been killing them and chucking them on verges to look like roadkill. The sett has been active for generations and he has worked out the path they take to their latrine, a hundred yards downstream. My remote camera set up is finally working, after months of engineering, building and polishing, mainly by retired design and technology teacher Chris. A DSLR perches inside a waterproof case, balanced on a stake in the ground. Two wireless flashes are positioned on either side, encased in camouflaged tupperware. A motion sensor is placed right next to the path in which I have buried ample amounts of peanut butter. Here is a species-selfie machine that mainly 'catches' mice, rats and pheasants. But after a couple of days, the badger ambles through at 8.55 pm on its way to the stream. Gotcha!

I find the bullfinches similarly elusive, having only managed to photograph them three times in the last two years. It's the colour of that pinkish breast on the male that always impresses but the beige female is, to my mind, equally as stylish.

Blackbird *Turdus merula* **on reflection pool:** Canon 1dx, 500 + 1.4x, 1/250 sec, F11, ISO 640, four Yongnuo flashes
Badger *Meles meles* **on path, nr Bishops Castle:** Canon 650d, 28mm, 1/100 sec, f8, ISO 800, flash, PIR sensor **Male Bullfinch** *Pyrrhula pyrrhula* **Bury Ditches:** Canon 7d2, 500mm + 2x, 1/400 sec, F8, ISO 400 **Female Bullfinch, Ludlow:** Canon 1dx, 500mm + 1.4x, 1/320 sec, F5.6, ISO 5000

Lapwing *Vanellus vanellus* **flock, Venus Pool:** *Canon 7d, 400mm, 1/1000 sec, F8, ISO 500* **Buzzard** *Buteo buteo* **flying in front of rainbow, Oakley Mynd:** *Canon 7d, 150-600mm, 1/400 sec, F7.1, ISO 160*

Buzzard

Were you made from a splatter of cloud mixed with mud?
When finished, then thrown against sky with a thud?
How you strain to gain height as you straddle the air,
or hunch on a branch with brooding-bright stare.
Often I hear you, your song on the breeze
is the cry of a cat as you prowl through the trees.
The crows shall harry like pestering aunts,
but peel off at last to return to their haunts.
Gamekeeper's poison is a feast for the night
and goshawk will have you and put out your light.

Yet once I saw twenty, all massed on a field.
When you flew, you were arrows, the sun as your shield.
The size of you, song of you, feather of art
as you swing through the hills and girdle my heart.

A good garden shot involves sleight of hand; hiding feeders and placing your bird in a pleasing position, but not through Photoshop. I search out fungus covered branches from the forest, use wire and screws to add it to my fence, space the feeders out so that there is room for birds to land, for me to focus on a pic that is simply bird and branch. Voila. The feeder is no more. Going further, I drill holes in the back of the branch and fill them with peanuts, all in mind of the visual impact, a stage manager conscious of what his audience might appreciate. I set up my tripod in the kitchen, in the way of anyone desperate for a cuppa. Kit fills our galley as I bend over the viewfinder like an old sailor swaying at sea with his sextant. The window has been cleaned on both sides, our house now a hide, the birds with no idea of my presence.

The final key is flash, four of them set like bright onlookers round the scene. The technical side is interesting as what the modern flash can do is dissect a slice of time, turning on and off again so quickly that motion is moulded to ice. Whatever that bird is up to at that very moment, becomes clarity. Wings as sharp as blades. Eyes like polished pebbles. Weather plays no part in it. Dark days and snowstorms only add to this intimate, domestic landscape.

When a blue tit flies over my tiny, Japanese rockery pond, the reflection and wing shape appear almost painted. That slice of time, frozen by flash, reveals what the human eye could never see. As Christmas approaches, my ongoing kitchen safari uncovers fighting goldfinches and the sharp claws of nuthatch, the underwing of a female woodpecker and the doubled up reflection of a peckish (shed-stored, tent-eating) wood mouse.

Goldfinches fighting in falling snow: Canon 1dx, 500mm + 1.4x, 1/200 sec, F11, ISO 400, 4 Yongnuo flashes **Long-tailed tit** *Aegithalos caudatus* **portrait:** Canon 1dx, 500mm + 1.4x, 1/200 sec, F13, ISO 160, 4 Yongnuo flashes **Male House sparrow** *Passer domesticus* **portrait:** Canon 1dx, 500mm + 1.4x, 1/4000 sec, F8, ISO 800, 4 Yongnuo flashes **Wood mouse** *Apodemus sylvaticus* **by pond:** Canon 1dx, 500mm, 1/250 sec, F11, ISO 640, 4 Yongnuo flashes **Blue tit** *Cyanistes caeruleus*: Canon 1dx, 500mm, 1/250 sec, F11, ISO 640, 3 Yongnuo flashes

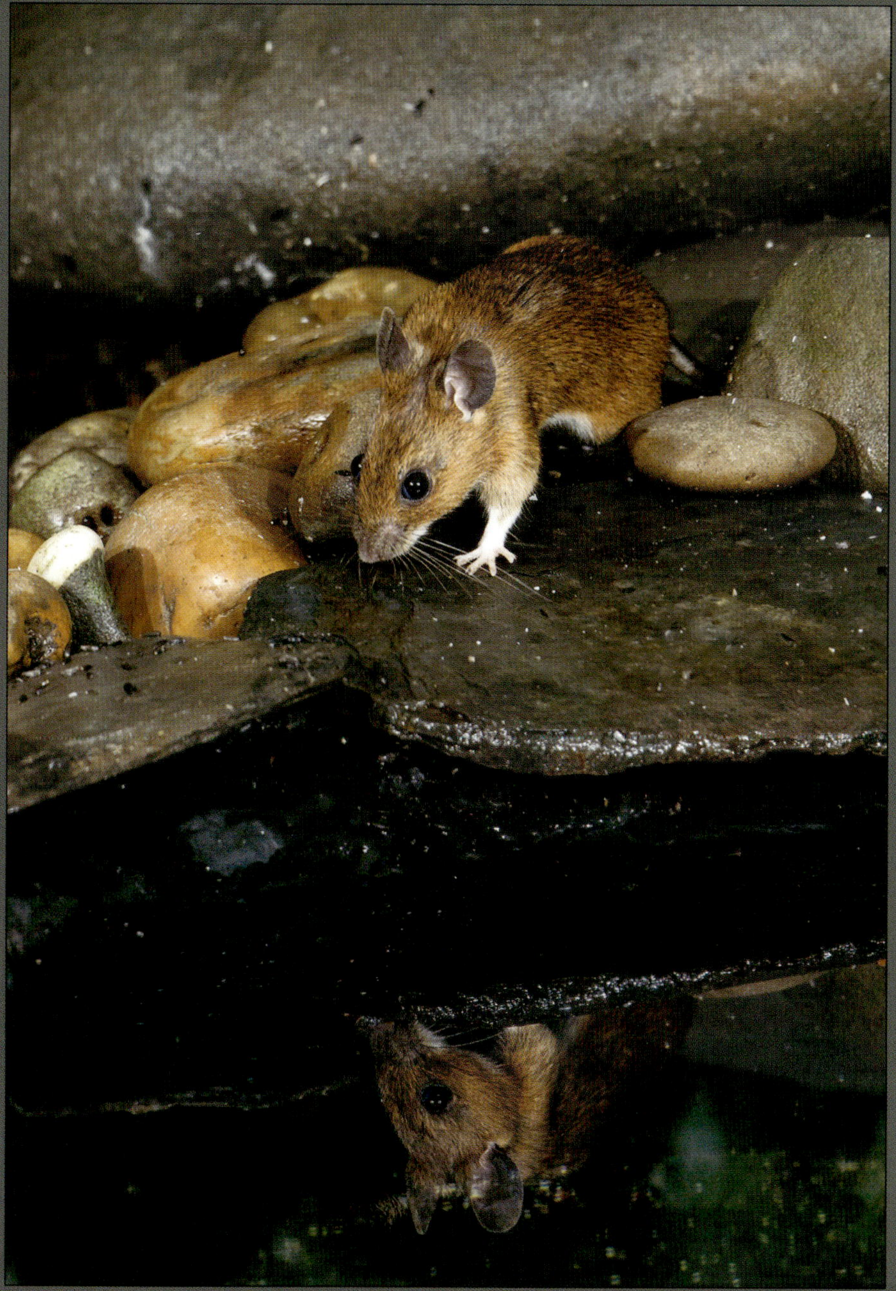

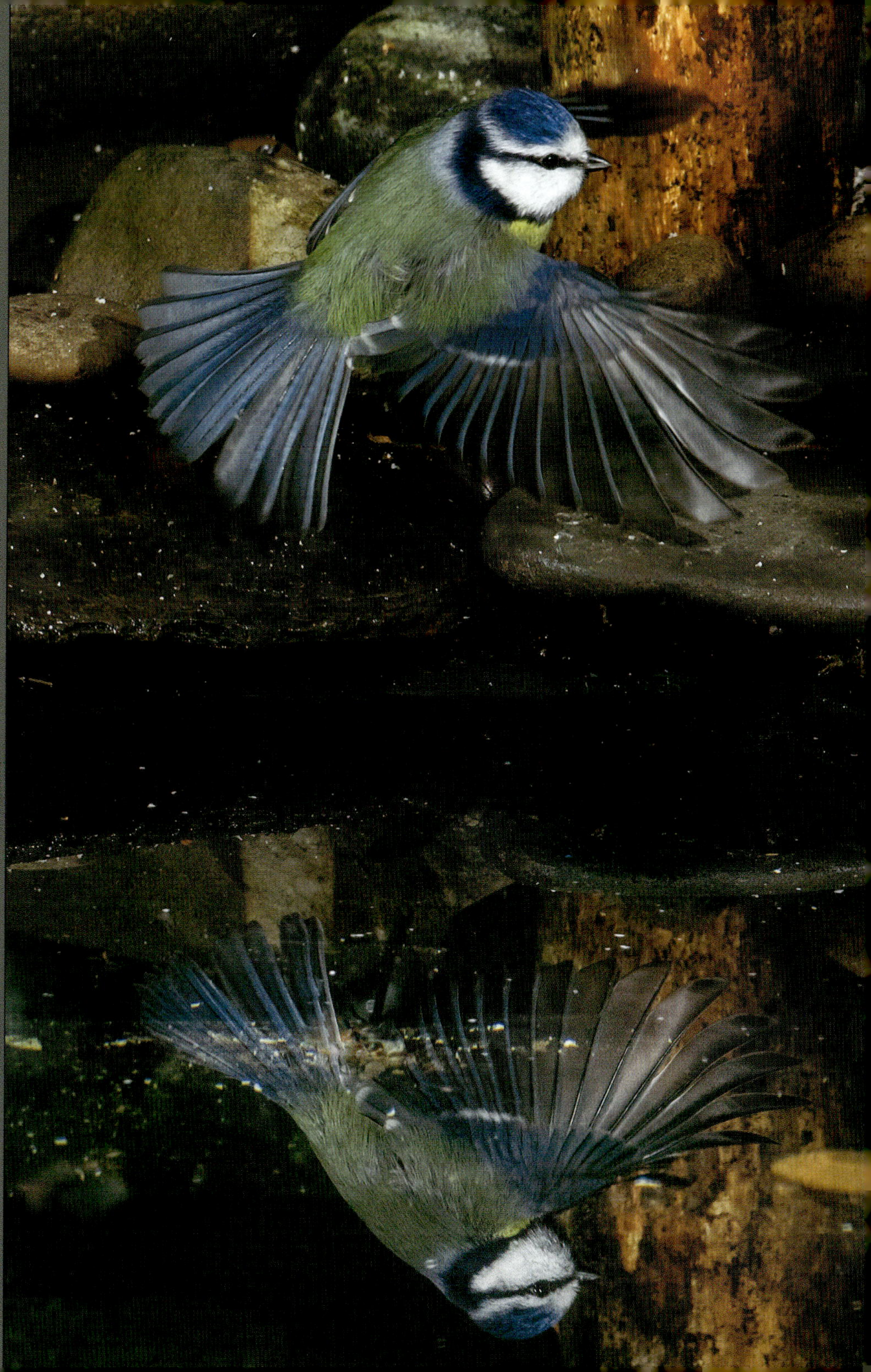

Stiperstones during January snow: Canon 6d, 16-35mm, 1/160 sec, F8, ISO 500, grad filters.
Close up of rocks looking towards Corndon Hill: Canon 6d, 16-35mm, 1/80 sec, F8, ISO 125, grad filters, tripod.

Hovering Kestrel *Falco tinnunculus*: Canon 7d2, 500mm + 2x, 1/1000 sec, F8, ISO 1250
Kestrel on roadkill: Canon 7d2, 500mm, 1/200 sec, F4, ISO 5000

32

Land and light in January are both etched and sharp. The lake I swim in at Pantglas, high on the Kerry Ridgeway, peopled by the ghosts of drovers long past, is now a frozen mirror. Strange to think that my summer swimming hole was created by a German bomber returning from the Liverpool raids during World War 2. Unused bombs needed to be jettisoned and this borderland idyll was the unintended target. Out of great destruction, nature has softened and filled history where a scar through the landscape takes on new meaning. The ancient fortified settlement of Caer Din Ring has no warriors now, nor even the echo of their boots. Only a smattering of gorse bushes and the far tint of a rainbow. Each visit I make to the solitude of these Shropshire uplands confirms that Barbados would be nice, but the borderlands have all that we need, if only we dare to look.

I have now moved my flat-pack hide to a woodland on the edge of the river Kemp. The acres here belong to Janet and Jeremy, who are more than happy for me to hang out and study the bird life of the trees. There is plenty to see, as I track wrens and tree-creepers through squelchy bog. With well-placed feeders and nuts hidden in the folds of the giant poplar trees, nuthatches and long-tailed tits are invited to my late winter table and the darting song thrush, sadly now in such decline it is a Red List species, crooks its neck to check me out.

Nuthatch *Sitta europaea*: Canon 7d2, 500mm + 1.4x, 1/1250 sec, F8, ISO 400 **Tree creeper** *Certhia familiaris*: Canon 7d2, 500mm + 1.4x, 1/2500 sec, F7.1, ISO 640 **Wren** *Troglodytes troglodytes*: Canon 7d2, 500mm + 1.4x, 1/1250 sec, F5.6, ISO 800 **Song thrush** *Turdus philomelos*: Canon 7d2, 500mm + 1.4x, 1/500 sec, F5.6, ISO 1600

A phone call comes from good mate Ric. Rumours of a certain, not-often seen bird have surfaced and he is keen we hunt such gossip down. The clouds that have made me so moody finally mooch off as I zip into the afternoon towards Wales. The chase is on! The edge of a massive roundabout in Welshpool is not quite Shangri-La. But Coed y Dinas has wealth hidden behind high hedges. The lake that lurks at the end of a good walk is lit up in this still-winter sun. At the hide, I meet a single exiteer who tells me that the bird in question was there earlier. Now it isn't. I satisfy myself with a resident snipe, feeding on its reflections at the water's edge.

Numbers grow – birders, gawkers, a young dad, with papoosed baby and a smattering of men and women with big lenses, all intent on one species. This bird comes into the reeds late on. At about 4.30 we catch our first glimpse. Everyone goes ogle-mad. But the reeds are frustrating – home for the bird, but a blur for all cameras. This is a type of heron, bulky and with long beak and prisoner-stripe feather patterns in multiple shades of brown to vanish into the reeds.

Feeding Snipe *Gallinago gallinago*: Canon 7d2, 500mm + 1.4x, 1/640 sec, F8, ISO 640 **Bittern** *Botaurus stellaris* **with mouth open:** Canon 1dx, 500mm, 1/500 sec, F4, ISO 1250 **Bittern portrait:** Canon 1dx, 500mm, 1/50 sec, F4, ISO 4000 **After sunset:** Canon 7d2, 500mm, 1/250 sec, F4, ISO 6400

The mood is good as best piccie spots are shared and there is a hushed banter while we all take in beauty. The hide fills with shadow and the last rays of light leave the lake. One by one, the crowd diminishes, though one of the birders says: 'wait and watch the bird rise.'

We wait. It does. Suddenly, there, clear in front of us, a bird that was extinct in the UK but has made some recovery. By now, it is almost hidden in the dark, but my camera works its magic, revealing the bird's own moony gold. The sun has fallen far behind the hills, turning the sky a deep orange and the horizon to a marching smudge of trees. Ric tells me he is so happy he made that call. Me too. Moon rising. Bittern rising. Not just in wilderness, but in Winter is Paradise now.

Wren *Troglodytes troglodytes* **at Venus Pool:** Canon 7d2, 500mm + 1.4x, 1/400 sec, F5.6, ISO 1600 **Snipe:** Canon 7d2, 500mm + 1.4x, 1/1600 sec, F5.6, ISO 2000 **Lapwing** *Vanellus vanellus* **with Canada goose** *Branta canadensis***:** Canon 7d, 150-600mm, 1/1250sec, F8, ISO 500

It's almost the end of winter, but one last snowfall surprises us all. The land is clenched in a still whiteness that persists for almost two weeks. On my regular walk to Walcot Lake, I bump into Tim, a birder who promptly turns me around and tells me to look into the neighboring field. One result of the long winter is a very hungry barn owl, who is right now quartering the frozen ploughed earth and grasses alongside for a bite of morning breakfast. This is rarity indeed. I have sometimes seen barn owl by night, a glaring gift of the dark, veering away from my headlights and into myth. There is also the potential of dusk and dawn, but the obviousness of this bird's needs amazes me. We spend twenty minutes together, Tim with his binoculars, me with my camera as the owl swoops, hovers, dives and finally comes into land on some nearby brash, claws out, a perfect touchdown moment I may never again see in my lifetime.

Barn owl *Tyto alba* **in snowy landscape:** Canon 650d, 55-250mm, 1/1000 sec, f9, ISO 200 **Barn owl diving:** Canon 650d, 55-250mm, 1/1600 sec, f5.6, ISO 200
Barn owl landing: Canon 650d, 55-250mm, 1/1000 sec, f7.1, ISO 200
Barn owl portrait: Canon 650d, 55-250mm, 1/250 sec, f14, ISO 200

Before dawn, I overlook Ludlow, the far Clee Hill a perfect silhouette trapped under an umbrella of impossible colour. It's going to be a good day, the first in ages. At the entrance to Mortimer forest, I meet up with Alan, the ranger. I have my camera, he, his gun and dog. The breeze is good, going against us as we climb a high ridge through mud and brambles. He spots a herd of female fallow grazing on the forestry track. Time to go quiet, stalk low, watch out for twigs. A nearby roe buck has smelt us, barks nervously. Alan only has moments to act. At the high point, he aims and fires, a crack like a tree breaking in a storm.

We scramble down. The other deer are gone, except for this female, taken with a single head shot. He cuts her open, pulls out the gralloch and carries it further down into the woods for scavengers. Then the heavy business of shifting and winching before we try one more stalking spot. On the way back, a raven with a smeared beak flares from the track, having already dined out. Back at the meat larder, next to the forestry office, the carcass has head and feet removed and is further stripped out. Glands are checked for TB, but this deer was healthy. Next stop, the gamedealer who then sells onto butchers and restaurants.

I have never been on a shoot or seen a cull. Neither have I been into a caged chicken 'farm' or deep litter unit. Alan is one of the most caring and knowledgeable conservationists I have ever met. He shows me the unruly brambles rearing between young trees and explains that these habitats are incredibly important for birds such as blackcaps and linnets. Deer are beautiful, but they also cause crop damage, endanger SSSIs and the ecology of our woodlands. If the deer grow too numerous (we have 1.5 million now in the UK), all this cover will be grazed out, as will new tree growth.

View over Ludlow at dawn: Canon 6d, 24-70mm, 1/30 sec, F3.2, ISO 12800 **Alan spotting for deer:** Canon 6d, 24-70mm, 1/40 sec, F2.8, ISO 250 **Deer carcass:** Canon 6d, 24-70mm, 1/100 sec, F4, ISO 500 **Lifting the carcass:** Canon 6d, 24-70mm, 1/160 sec, F2.8, ISO 320 **Portrait with carcass:** Canon 6d, 24-70mm, 1/200 sec, F2.8, ISO 500

Without natural predators like wolves, or lynxes, foresters work on creating balance in the eco-system. The result? Food miles are negligible as I take my wife out to eat at the perfectly named Mortimer's in town. The main course is venison, taken from these very woods, probably by Alan, and now given an award by the Slow Food Ark of Taste. These deer have a wild life – far better than most intensively reared livestock and poultry in the UK that we are happy to pick up pre-packaged in the supermarket.

There is a reason Alan kills mainly females. Once the herd strays off forestry land, (though in the case of poachers this boundary does not exist), most shooters like to take out bucks and stags. The sad thing, and Alan has seen it, is that if there is a herd of bucks, a shooter will often pick the biggest and healthiest with the largest antlers – a specimen that, come the rutting season, would ensure the health of the herd. So the cruellest predator is, as ever, unthinking man.

The dark days are coming to a close. The snow has gone leaving only its echo in pools of dawn field frost. The hares are growing frisky, sniffing out the blossoming that is to come. I have finally discovered two ways to approach a hare. The first is on hands and knees, slowly, with no threat. The hare knows it can run at any time but this one almost went to sleep in front of me. The other involves stillness. Stand for long enough and you might be mistaken for a tree. It works to the extent that hare runs right past me, out of winter and straight into spring.

Two hares portrait: Canon 1dx, 500mm + 2x, 1/1600 sec, F8, ISO 1000 **Hare close up:** Canon 6d, 150-600, 1/1250 sec, F8, ISO 3200 **Running hare:** Canon 7d, 150-600, 1/1250 sec, F8, ISO 1600

The Hare Whisperer

At dawn, the light is tinted low
As if the sun were leavening the day
    to a risen yeast.
And here are the hares, wild with greenery
    bubbling earth bursting through limb and paw
As they leap, run perfect rings that were ritual
    before Stonehenge.

Hare of the hind legs, first of pistons,
Driven hare, heaving hare of the lollop,
    gainer of air with an ease.

This is a yearly catch can that shall lead to
A flummox of paws, a head battering-ram
As buck and doe duke it out for who
    shall have the pleasure,
For if fox does not have his beget
    in the form as polished as shell, new life-leveret.

I am the tall tree, ignored,
As hare after hare runs, no, sprints, no,
    as the peregrine falls in a stoop,
So hare, horizontal, negotiates distance,
    until he is whisker,
Amber of eye,
    pressed pine sap of aeons
    washed up on this furred shore.

Almost in my face
Swerves by my boots with a grace,
Then slipping like down-dark tree roots
To a low land only hinted at in
    tinted dreams as I shifted in my form
Far, and far again before dawn.

Spring

I always feel a relief when the dark days of winter give way to a softening. As a family, we've hunkered at home with box sets and heating, or scurried to and from work and shops. Meanwhile, the birds and animals were ensconced in trees, hedges, or lay low under earth, their heartbeats slowed as winds scraped bare branches. Now, there are buds, bees and bounce. Hares rear up, filled with energy and the first lambs are properly bonkers as they leap about at Walcot Lake. Grass snakes swim free from hibernation at Venus Pool while marsh tits sing for the spring at Kempton. The otters at Bridgnorth are feeding up, providing dawn commuters, walkers and photographers with the sight of pure wildness by a city centre bridge. Up on the Stiperstones, when good people are abed, I have outstayed my welcome, watching as evening lights up the far Welsh hills, glad that the cotton-grass has returned to this upland. As night comes on and my fingers lose feeling, the stars shyly gather until their numbers make a Milky Way. I wish that the light leaching over the horizon were the last of day, and not the flared, fluorescent light pollution from Shrewsbury.

Closer to home, robins and blackbirds brave corners of local garden sheds to make new families. There are other, more difficult stories that give hope and cause concern. Due to modern farming practices, skylark numbers have been nationally decimated. Here in Shropshire, they hang on in the high places, small singing barometers of natural health which must be celebrated and preserved. The lesser-spotted woodpecker is sadly and aptly named. Once common in the county, they are now hardly ever spotted. The pair I was honoured to see feeding their young in a dead tree stump survive on a tiny reserve behind a Telford housing estate. Feathers and colour among concrete and tarmac.

The uplands are the larder of a Shropshire we must keep well stocked. Without places such as the Long Mynd and the Stiperstones, dwindling species could easily be lost. Here, alongside the countless meadow pipits and good skylark numbers, are ravens and wheatears, stonechats now setting out territory as each male proclaims to listening females that he is the brightest and boldest. All is change. On sunny mornings at the top of the Mynd, the male red grouse with his arched postbox-red eyebrow has already paired with a female. New life waits in the feathered wings. The season is brought to a finale by a burst of breeding colour that has eluded me for years. After days in a hide, to see kingfisher land in front of me is an honour that sets heart racing, and fingers shaking. Here is vibrance, life, hope, effort, all contained in one river-racing perfect package, a most stunning symbol of spring.

Brown Hare *Lepus europaeus*
Mears Barn: Canon 7d2, 500mm,
ISO 1250, 1/1600 sec f4 **Lambs**
Ovis aries **Walcot Lake:** Canon 7d,
Tamron 150-600mm, ISO 800 1/1600
sec f6.3 **Honey bee** *Apis mellifera*
**in my back garden, Lydbury
North:** Canon 1dx, 100mm macro,
ISO 3200, 1/5000 sec, f5.6

Jonathan with struggling lamb:
Canon 1dx, 100mm macro, ISO 100,
1/800 sec f2.8 **Jonathan wiping
lamb under heat lamp:** Canon
1dx, 100mm macro, ISO 100, 1/500
sec f4. **Lamb portrait:** Canon 1dx,
50mm 1.4, ISO 100, 1/250 sec f1.4

M y friend Caroline's brother, Jonathan has
been farming for generations on the hill
behind Bishop's Castle. Spring, for him
means long nights of lambing and keeping a sharp eye
on the fields by the farmhouse. Today, his concern pays
off, as one little lamb is struggling in the damp weather.
Jonathan takes her off the field. The carrying seems
cruel but that's where a photo sometimes needs an
explanation, mainly provided by how relaxed the mother
is as she trots alongside. The farmer is about his work,
wiping the lamb down, putting her gently under the heat
lamp and giving her life's best chance. When I go back
two weeks later, this has turned into a happy spring
story. The lamb is well and Jonathan's flock increased.

My first ever grass snake. Do I track it for days through wild fens, listening for slithering? No. But I do follow the sound of excited shutter clicks at Venus Pool, as a veritable paparazzi of keen clickers ogle this reptilian star. My field skills pay off as water makes the moment, giving me two snakes for the price of one!

Grass snake, *Natrix natrix* **Venus Pool, Shrewsbury:** Canon 7d, Tamron 150-600, ISO 800, 1/600 sec f8 **Lapwing** *Vanellus vanellus*, **Venus Pool, Shrewsbury:** Canon 7d2, 500mm+1.4x, ISO 400, 1/1600 sec f8

When my neighbours Eileen and Derek tell me they have tree sparrows in their garden, I try not to profess my doubts. This little bird has declined dramatically. Now, for every fifty house sparrows, you get one tree sparrow, if you are lucky. And I am, as I crouch near their hedgerow to snap this intimate portrait. How to tell the difference? One easy marker is that lovely black spot under the eye, almost like a pair of sideburns as well as a chestnut-coloured cap on their head.

Marsh Tit *Poecile palustris*, **Kempton:** Canon 7d2, 500mm+1.4x, ISO 1600, 1/500 sec f5.6
Tree Sparrow *Passer montanus*, **Oakley Mynd:** Canon 7d2, 500mm+1.4x, ISO 800, 1/640 sec f8

My mate Robin rings up to tell me there are otters on the river Severn at Bridgnorth. This is after months of putting out cam-trail cameras at river spots near Church Stretton and Welshpool. I've caught blurry, infra red shots of these sleek fishing machines from a remotely triggered gizmo, but it isn't the same as getting up close and viewing in real time. Otter numbers have improved in the last few years and they are now in every river in Shropshire. I, like many Salopians, had never seen a single otter in its watery habitat. 7am is the time, the pattern being a feeding journey either side of Low Town Bridge. I rise early, coffee-flasked and bleary-eyed to drive through the dark, only to acquire the moon, some geese and chats with other keen snappers. Several visits later, persistence pays off with whoops of joy and gangs of us running up and down riverbanks to focus on a very relaxed otter, almost putting on a show for us. I'm not complaining, for here, in the heart of town, as lorries rumble by, is the most sinuous of swimmers, elegantly adapted to the flow and fall of the Severn. As I treat myself to a very nice fry up in the café on the bridge afterwards, I can see I've caught a glimpse of that free spirit. Wahay!

Bridgnorth before dawn: Canon 1dx, 70-200mm, ISO 800, 1/800 sec at f4 **Otter** *Lutra lutra* **swimming:** Canon 1dx, 500mm+1.4x, ISO 1600 1/1250 sec f5.6 **Emden Goose** *Anser anser*, **Bridgnorth:** Canon 1dx, 500mm+1.4x, ISO 500 1/800 sec f5.6

Otter with fish and eye portrait: Canon
1dx, 500mm + 1.4x, 1/1000 sec, F 5.6, ISO
2000 **Otter with lit up fish:** Canon 1dx,
500mm+1.4x, ISO 1600 1/2000 sec f5.6
Otter with head shot: Canon 1dx, 500mm
+ 1.4x, 1/1600 sec, F 5.6, ISO 2000

Convincing my wife I need a new lens requires weeks of tactical pleading. She finally relents, not caring for my explanation that the wonders of the heavens can only be captured with a wide-angle Samyang lens. This clear April night I want to see what the Stiperstones can offer. Though the valleys are warming up, no-one has informed the exposed quartzite outcrops that a new season is in play. Layered up, I carry my kit over ankle-snatching paths to a point where land meets sky. A solid tripod is a must, as is a full-frame camera body that can cope with high ISO. Camera manual focused on infinity at f2.8, remote cable to stop camera shake, then wait for twilight to fade and stars to dazzle. A curlew cries past, a sudden flare in the near darkness. I feel delightfully alone aside from the far turning on of farm lights and creeping cars. Emerging on my screen, is a still-life lightscape in a barren and high hide out.

Milky Way, Stiperstones: Canon 6d,
Samyang 14mm f2.8, ISO 3200, 23 sec, f2.8
**Stiperstones at sunset with Common
cotton-grass** *Eriophorum angustifolium***:**
Canon 6d, 16-35mm f4, ISO 640, 1/160 sec f8

W ho would know that the smallest bird in Europe, which is surprisingly common, lives right in our village churchyard? Before I was interested in photography I had never seen one. The Goldcrest likes conifers, hence the graveyard association. They are also one of the few birds who respond to bird calls. When I put my phone on a gravestone and turn it on to play the male's song, a real male quickly darts out to see off the challenger, raising its incredible yellow crest in aggression. I have to be quick as they jump about vigorously, but for me the excitement is easily up there with the dawn I came upon a cheetah kill in Kenya. There is stunning wildlife under our noses, and these borderlands have changed before my eyes as I slowly delve into their secrets.

Goldcrest *Regulus regulus* **with wings raised:** Canon 7d2, 500mm f4, ISO 640, 1/2500 sec f6.3 **Goldcrest on branch with buds:** Canon 7d2, 500mm f4, ISO 800, 1/800 sec f4 **Goldcrest with crest raised:** Canon 7d2, 500mm f4, ISO 2500, 1/2500 sec f6.3

I can quite understand why Jim is protective of his blackbirds. Each year they favour his shed in the corner of a hidden patio in Bishop's Castle. As we creep out of the back door of his house, I can hear the cries of the young. Jim informs me I can only stay for a few minutes as he does not want the birds disturbed. So, I quickly set up my tripod outside the window where the mother is flying in with food every few minutes. Remote attached, I retreat and pray. The mother is not bothered by this new metal shiny tree – she has a job to do. I have had several offers to help me 'Photoshop' the bottle out. But why? It tells the story. They have adapted to live among us. In this instance, that relationship gloriously works.

Even more with the robins – from sheds in Clungunford, and Aston Munslow where my good friend Lynne has some very boisterous dogs. This corner of her outbuilding is totally exposed and yet life continues. The word 'brave' is right. For here among clutter and canine jumping around, the male robin is about his work, presenting his partner with a crane fly that looks like a work of Fabergé-enamelled bling.

Robin *Erithacus rubecula* **with cranefly** *Tipula paludosa*: Canon 1dx, 500mm f4, ISO 800, 1/160 sec, f11, multiple flash
Robin with worm: Canon 7d, 70-200mm f2.8, ISO 1600, 1/200 sec, f4 **Blackbird** *Turdus merula* **mother in shed:** Canon 6d, Tamron 150-600, ISO 3200, 1/200 sec f8, tripod, remote release

A pair of Great crested grebes *Podiceps cristatus*,
Darnford Lake: Canon 1dx, 500mm f4 + 2x, ISO 800,
1/1600 sec, f8 **Coot** *Fulica atra* **and chick, Walcot Lake:**
Canon 1dx, 500mm f4 + 1.4x, ISO 640, 1/1250 sec, f8

U p above Totterton, on friendly farmer's land, I am also the early bird, walking to catch this blue dawn light. My footsteps are enough to scatter the skylarks, who rise in loops, with strange mid-air pauses as if to gather breath for their song. I am glad of them, happy to be their visual champion this morning as they fill the hills with their rising harmonies.

When I tell my birder friend Pete about an encounter with lesser-spotted woodpeckers, he is for once flabbergasted. He hasn't seen one in decades in Shropshire and reckons there are now only 30-40 pairs in the whole county, whereas once they were common. My good grace is entirely thanks to fellow photo-nut Tim who has spent the last few years tracking the wildlife in the hidden reserves of Telford. This spot behind a housing estate, a miracle of wilderness, is yards from the world of roundabouts and boxed-up modern housing. The high hollow hole of a dead tree is a perfect spot for the parents to raise their young who are both demanding and hungry. A wonderful way to spend a morning, though by the end my neck and back are in agony from the bend to focus upwards. I love their garnet eyes, such a red bauble. That, with almost designer-vivid markings, makes up a perfect pecking package.

Skylark *Alauda arvensis* **at Totterton:**
Canon 7d, Tamron 150-600mm, ISO
1000, 1/2500 sec, f8 **Lesser-spotted
woodpeckers** *Dendrocopos minor* **all:**
Canon 1dx, 500mm f4 + 1.4x, ISO 1250,
1/2500 sec, f8

Raven *Corvus corax* **on the Long Mynd:** Canon 1dx,
500mm f4 + 1.4x, ISO 800, 1/2500 sec, f6.3
Wheatear *Oenanthe oenanthe* **at dawn, Stiperstones:**
Canon 7d2, 500mm f4, ISO 640, 1/400 sec, f8

Female skylark, Stiperstones: Canon 7d2, 500mm f4,
ISO 500, 1/2000 sec, f5.6   **Male skylark with crest
raised and worm, Stiperstones:** Canon 7d2, 500mm f4
+ 1.4x, ISO 1000, 1/1600 sec, f5.6

Grey wagtail *Motacilla cinerea* **at Lightspout Hollow Waterfall, Long Mynd:** Canon 1dx, 500mm f4 + 1.4x, ISO 1000, 1/2500 sec, f5.6 **Male stonechat** *Saxicola torquata*, **Long Mynd:** Canon 1dx, 500mm f4 + 1.4x, ISO 500, 1/2000 sec, f5.6 **Green Hairstreak butterfly** *Callophrys rubi*, **Stiperstones:** Canon 6d, 100mm macro, ISO 320, 1/160 sec, f10, ringflash

The red grouse has eluded me for months. My employers at the National Trust and Natural England are keen for close ups and context shots, but my only photo so far has been a popped up head above far off heather. On this bright morning, I am out with my very first client who is wanting to photograph Long Mynd wildlife. I have no idea why she is paying me as the grouse has done its best to avoid me so far and I am sure she would not be interested in a few crows and sheep. However, today the gods of small game are in my favour. As I drive to meet her just after sunrise, a male red grouse is strutting around the verge and even along the road as if on the way to work. A most elegant commuter indeed, who later shows how well adapted to heather he is as his head melds with the colours of the landscape. My client is content and all is well.

Red grouse *Lagopus lagopus* **on road:** Canon 1dx, 500mm f4 + 1.4x, ISO 1000, 1/2500 sec, f5.6 **Red grouse portrait:** Canon 1dx, 500mm f4 + 1.4x, ISO 1000, 1/2500 sec, f5.6 **Red grouse hidden in heather:** Canon 1dx, 500mm f4 + 1.4x, ISO 1000, 1/2000 sec, f8

Red Game

I have spent months not believing in you. If you were
    a religion I would be biblical in my atheism.

When clear night felled the warmth of day high
    in the ridged Stiperstones, your call
was an affront to comfort,
    both braying and ghostish as it faded.

That was all, apart from the odd pop-up eyebrow
    a great quizzical red that was hard to separate from heather,
a partial and unmiraculous vision.

To say you dissolved into the landscape as I approached
    would be an insult to sugar.
Your vanishing left me longing for the sweetness of sight.

Silly me. Months, as I said, of carousing through non-pathy
    landscape where every bit of growth made a beeline
from boot to sock.

I suffered in my search, like some forlorn pilgrim,
    still without faith, traipsing dawn and dusk,
the stubborn path of my ancestors.

Of course you avoided me, my kind. Knowing history
    and your ancient title of 'red game', so would I.

This seems to be the way of it. The more effort,
    the less of happenstance. Until this dawn,
where I am alone on the Mynd
    except for an early and most keen cyclist.

My eyes, as ever, on the prowl. Maybe a skylark if I am lucky,
    a pipit if not. Then, and it is both sudden and unexpected,
You appear before me, perhaps as He would,
    pecking heather, rather relaxed
all the glory of gold, tabards of red in your plumage.
    You pause, eat, stroll across the road
as if commuting,
    probably not aware how brilliant and rare you are.

I have no choice but to hang my disbelief on a hook.
    There's evidence in your bulbous eye,
the ridiculous slash of red, the white feathering round your
    sturdy workman's legs.

And when you fly, cry out to the whole of Shropshire,
    I see that I no longer need to pray
    Nor grouse about this far and shining day.

It is an understatement to say I am obsessed with light. For me, it is a medium through which I engage with what flies and stands and stares. My local heron at Walcot is probably sick of being snapped and how was it to know the early sun would cut across its face? As for the orange patch – is it the reflection of Walcot Hall's historic brickwork, or some early flowering plant? Middle age means I can't remember and the camera is not that advanced to google eyesight.

Dusk brings its own gifts: my friend, Natural England ranger Simon, is driving me back from an evening shoot on the Stiperstones. As we delve into the woods behind Linley, he turns the engine off and we coast to a halt. His shoulder becomes my tripod and my camera is taken to the limits of its settings as a young roe buck stares out of the dimness. We are in his lands now, and long may he laugh and leap over the concept of ownership and fences, enclosure and privacy. If only we could return the humbleness of being custodians rather than rapacious controllers and diminishers of this shrinking wilderness.

Grey heron *Ardea cinerea*, Walcot Lake:
Canon 7d2, 500mm f4, ISO 1250, 1/2500
sec, f4. **Roe buck** *Capreolus capreolus*,
Linley: Canon 1dx, 500mm f4 + 1.4×, ISO
25600, 1/160 sec, f5.6

I have been kindly invited to Soulton Hall, north of Shrewsbury, by Tim Ashton to stay, and be fed and watered in return for walking the land and seeing what I can find. At last the bluebells have arrived and what better place to reveal their rich and verdant glory? With them, the woods undergo transubstantiation of the best sort, from the muddy waters of winter to the bouquet, the heady colours, the draft that I drink in the deep dusk of spring. Dawn brings the best moment, as a feeding fox stops to stare at the tall stranger in its territory. We meet for an instant until he lopes off through peaty-brown ploughed fields.

Bluebell *Hyacinthoides non-scripta* **portrait:** Canon 6d, 16-35mm f4, ISO 125, 1/80 sec, f8 **Red fox** *Vulpes vulpes* **in the fields at dawn:** Canon 1dx, 500mm f4 + 1.4x, ISO 500, 1/1000 sec, f5.6 **Dandelion** *Taraxacum officinale* **at dawn:** Canon 6d, 16-35mm f4, ISO 200, 1/40 sec, f10, grad filters

Dipper *Cinclus cinclus*, **Ludlow:** Canon 1dx, 500mm f4 + 1.4x, ISO 25600, 1/160 sec, f5.6 **Female kingfisher** *Alcedo atthis* **portrait:** Canon 1dx, 500mm f4 + 2x, ISO 640, 1/800 sec, f8

River birds are sometimes hard to spot. The dipper's up and down bobbing often melds into the pebbles and rocks it hunts around. Once in a while, breeding makes behaviour more approachable, as with this dipper at Ludlow's Millenium Green, whose nest is right under the weir, walked over the top of by teenagers, parents and children, mad wild swimmers and the odd photographer.

The dipper is a special bird, but, there has always been one river dweller I dreamed of. I once bought my wife a necklace of Lapis Lazuli beads – each with a hue that seemed to contain the circumference of the sky. No wonder the Old Masters ground the stone for their paint. If only they could have distilled the feathers of a kingfisher.

What had I seen of this river bird as I went for my wild swims? A zip of intense colour so fast it was said to be able to ward off Zeus's lightning. As a fledgling photographer, I'd sat in official hides on well-known reserves where my skill netted me a blur on a stick.

Until I met my good friend Alan. This man has an army history as extraordinary as many of the creatures he patiently stalks. He understands how each pair commands a kilometre of river along with known perching and fishing spots. With him, I have walked soft through woods, set up camouflaged hides that gave the best view over their watery A-Z. Just as we like our favourite coffee shop on a certain day or hour, so kingfisher will come back to a perch like clockwork if undisturbed.

Getting close is my grail, to shrink that far blur into a still life. Days of endless patience, where nothing happens, the camera doesn't focus in time, or kingfisher decides a perch round the river bend is a better spot.

On this particular day after three hours of cramp and missed opportunities, I am weeping with frustration. But we have friends for a reason, and Alan literally pokes me in the stomach and tells me to 'think'. It calms me. We carry on. Him buried by a tree with a net over his body, me in my pop-up tent on the pebbles of the river bank.

Kingfisher comes down, the lapis of the earth ground into his wings, crazy close. He knows I am there, but is not bothered. About his business, this glorious male with a huge stickleback. Not far away, the fledglings are ready to be fed, and it turns out, fly the nest that next morning. For now, he poses with the sky on his back. King of the fishers – as the poet Frederick William Faber said *'There came, Swift as a meteor's shining flame, A kingfisher from out on the brake, And almost seemed to leave a wake, Of brilliant hues behind.'*

Male kingfisher showing back: Canon 1dx, 500mm f4, ISO 250, 1/800 sec, f4
Male kingfisher on clay bank with stickleback: Canon 1dx, 500mm f4, ISO 1250, 1/800 sec, f8 **Male kingfisher taking off:** Canon 7d2, 500mm f4, ISO 800, 1/650 sec, f4

Summer

Who would have thought that summer might begin in my carport, where a shallow scallop of stone is topped by a high holly and elder hedge? Sandwiched in-between, I spy a wren's nest. So, I start the season sitting on my neighbour's verge for hours, hoping to catch a glimpse of the young fledglings. A pattern of insect-bearing parents helps me hone in on the spot where I must set my lens, and sit for hours to celebrate a brave new life in my back yard. Everywhere, the light astounds me, from the sunsets west of the Stiperstones that rival any Lake District view, to the morning mist that blankets beneath the Long Mynd. Dawn arrives so early now that I must nail myself to my iphone alarm, mustering hope in the pre-morn gloom that long drives and hurling myself about the landscape will be worth it. It always is, for then the county feels as if it belongs to me, my aloneness exhilarating as I watch the sun come into being. In my exploration, near at hand seems to be the place to go – at the top of our hill, in a cluster of houses, my neighbour John points out the coconut shell that he nailed to his shed. There are breathing miracles within: of the flycatcher variety. On the roof of our Victorian converted chapel, a young swallow waits with head up for mother to swing by, using the sky as a flying-insect larder. These are the months of increase in Shropshire and beyond. On Corndon Hill, in my friend Wendy Jane's family cottage, a redstart nests in a crack in the wall using architecture, the built landscape, as a bolthole. Young frogs make a massive migration measured in metres, across a footpath and into the safety of Walcot lake. To see them jump many times their height puts our own Olympic efforts into perspective.

This is a summer of firsts: my first ever green woodpecker, vibrant and verdant and only yards from the public hide at Venus Pools; my first hobby gliding at giddy speed over the Mynd; my first up-close and personal mink, who dives into the river I am emerging from at Beambridge. Whatever your opinion on this brutal predator, this is an incredible encounter.

The best of the season lies in wait. Suddenly, the Mynd and Stiperstones, those great Shropshire uplands, transform from rich brown to a velvety purple. The heather has blossomed and my National Trust friend and employer Pete Carty lays down his gauntlet: 'Every wildlife shot you previously got, Andy, now I want you to achieve the same, but with that lovely heather background.' No pressure there then. I become addicted to these high ridgeways, venturing out at dawn, midday and dusk over and over. Ravens, meadow pipits and red grouse thankfully oblige.

Night also gives new gifts. The technique I developed for photographing the Milky Way has been polished and I finally find a proper dark-skies spot on Nipstone. Although the stars are fab, the rock and vegetation also deserve its place in my portrait. With a thirty second exposure, I have time to light paint the foreground with a cheapy LED eBay special. All for art's sake.

Night is also the time when another shy creature comes out. After months of planning, I have caught her, the moon, rising above the Devil's Chair.

Slowly, the heather loses its vibrancy. The dragonflies hang on as bracken burns to brown and leaves curl. The heatwave that has gone on and on, doesn't anymore and change is in the air. Still, this has been a summer of sweetness, of all things, and creatures blossoming anew.

Stiperstones at sunset with gorse *Ulex europeaus*:
Canon 6d, 16-35mm, 1/125 sec, f8 ISO 400
Fledgling wren *Troglodytes troglodytes*, **Lydbury North:** Canon 7d2, 500mm, 1/250 sec, f8 ISO 640
Lapwing *Vanellus vanellus* **in flight:** Canon 7d2, 500mm, 1/2000 sec, f4, ISO 200

Sometimes, as I drive back late from Ludlow, like a lone vehicular mariner, the small country roads appear to elongate. There are corners and trees I do not know. In amongst this strangeness, if I am blessed, a white shape unexpectedly shifts through the shadows. Each time I see a barn owl, I know this is my good-omen bird come into being. Little do I realize that my efforts to search out and photograph will be eased by my neighbour Kerm who informs me that one of these delightful creatures roosts in a tree not two fields away from me. I'm doubtful, having lived in our family house for twenty years, but go to look at said tree at the right time – dusk. There! A paleness among the summer greenery! Long lenses, much patience and several dawn and after-day visits finally give me the glimpses I dreamed of.

Could it only be by chance,
    The wonder of your white-night dance?
This shadow I can barely trace –
    A shooting star with feathered grace.
Mighty owl, in you I see
    An echo of eternity.

Barn owl *Tyto alba* **portrait in tree at dusk:** Canon 1dx, 500mm + 1.4x, 1/640 sec, f5.6, ISO 2500
Barn owl flying at dusk: Canon 1dx, 500mm, 1/1000 sec, f4, ISO 8000
Barn owl in tree hollow: Canon 7d2, 500mm + 1.4x, 1/320 sec, f5.6, ISO 1250

I am out for owls again – it can become an obsession, and I heard rumours of little owls at Totterton. Sadly, I spend way too much time wandering sunken lanes turned into tunnels by beech tree canopies. At the end of one such lane, my neighbour John is working on his car. He has seen owls, yes, but not right now. However, if I lift my eyes towards the coconut shell he's nailed to the top of his shed, I might discover something even more exciting. Life will out. Or rather, life will find a comfy, small, dark, safe place and make new life within. The spotted flycatcher pair have squeezed their brood into this space, which they are rapidly out-growing. Over the next few days, I watch the imperatives of feeding, of hope and of new wings being stretched, ready for first flight. Numbers are a sixth of what they were thirty years ago, so any help we can give them should be applauded. I never won a coconut at the fair back in my 1970's youth, but today, the prize is right in front of me.

Spotted flycatcher *Muscicapa striata* **brood, Totterton:**
Canon 1dx, 500mm + 1.4x, 1/640 sec, f8, ISO 3200
Spotted flycatcher mother feeding fledgling, Totterton:
Canon 1dx, 500mm + 1.4x, 1/500 sec, f5.6, ISO 16000
Spotted flycatcher fledgling trying out wings, Totterton:
Canon 1dx, 500mm + 1.4x, 1/400 sec, f8, ISO 2000

At Venus Pool, darting in and out of the reeds, the reed warbler is about its business. It catches hoverflies, while I try to catch it – with both my 500 lens and a double extender giving me 1000mm of reach. But this has the same effect as a very long, unstable telescope – the longer the distance, the greater the difficulty of focus. The raft spider at Whixall Moss lies at the opposite end of the spectrum. Now, I have to get close in with a 100 mm macro lens. This involves me lying down on wet boggy ground and inching myself right out over the edge of the pool to try and focus a few millimetres from the spider, while aiming to keep the camera steady. I'm amazed I don't fall in, and also amazed to see I have caught the spider mid meal, with a constellation of waterborne insects standing around on the water's surface like spectators.

Wood Lane reserve, near Ellesmere, is a former industrial site that now plays host to a variety of species, including up to 500 pairs of breeding sand martins in the vast, man-made sand dunes. During a day of ringing, when vast, billowing nets are put up to catch the birds, I have the honour of seeing a martin up close. Ringing and tagging are essential work, helping us to understand what is happening to creatures in the places they live and how this affects population increases and decreases. Today, I see that work done with both sensitivity and commitment.

Reed warbler *Acrocephalus scirpaceus***, Venus Pool:** Canon 1dx, 500mm + 2x, 1/1250 sec, f8, ISO 640 **Raft spider** *Dolomedes plantarius***, Whixall Moss:** Canon 1dx, 100mm macro, 1/200 sec, f10, ISO 1000 **Sand martin** *Ripana ripana* **ringing, Wood Lane Reserve:** Canon 1dx, 500m, 1/1250 sec, f4, ISO 400 **Sand martin weighing:** Canon 6d, 17-40mm, 1/2500 sec, f4, ISO 1000 **Sand martin portrait with hand:** Canon 1dx, 500mm, 1/1250 sec, f4, ISO 400 **Sand martin claw ring:** Canon 1dx, 500mm, 1/800 sec, f4, ISO 400 **Industrial workings:** Canon 6d, 17-40mm, 1/500 sec, f4, ISO 100 **Netting in front of nest holes:** Canon 1dx, 500mm, 1/1250 sec, f4, ISO 400

I am but mad north-north-west. When the wind is southerly,
I know a hawk from a handsaw [Heron]

Hamlet Act 2: Scene 2

Jemmy Lang Legs

What do you spy from your spot on the bank
Jemmy Heron, Moll Hern, Diddleton Frank

Neck stretched out in a wood-turned curl
Jack Hern, Skip Hegrie, Frank Hanser, Tammie Herl

All of you stillness, like a grey ship-wreck
Joan na-ma-crank, Harnsey, Long Neck

The sun in your eye, as you stoop at the shore
Herald, Jemmy Lang Legs, Long Necky, Heronshaw

Dive is so sudden and your beak in the burn
Hernsey, Hernsaw, Varn, Yarn and Ern

Carp for your supper, well done Jenny Crow
Longnix, Huron, Harn, Hironceau.

At Walcot on a sunny afternoon, I spy the local heron in the middle of the lake. I have been reading about the behaviour of birds before they take flight – how buzzards, which I have now observed and understand, often lift their tail feathers like an old maiden's skirts and defecate before taking to the air. With heron, as I settle in to watch, there is intention, a slight lean forward. My settings are right, and my focus locked on as it grabs the sky, vast ungainly wings slow at first to achieve the necessary body height, but once they do, it is most elegant. Fast shutter speed freezes motion, not only catches heron doubled up, followed by a reflected under-ghost, but the moment as a wing clips the water, its little splash almost turned to ice. There is a great sense of purpose in its eye, the evolutionary perfection of forward wing, feather, streamlined body and claws trailing behind in the slipstream.

Heron with large tench *Tinca tinca*, **Walcot Lake:** Canon 1dx, 500mm + 1.4x, 1/1250 sec, f5.6, ISO 400 **Jumping juvenile toad** *Bufo bufo***, Walcot Lake:** Canon 1dx, 100mm macros, 1/4000 sec, f8, ISO 3200 **Heron, Walcot Lake:** Canon 1dx, 500mm + 1.4x, 1/2000 sec, f5.6, ISO 800

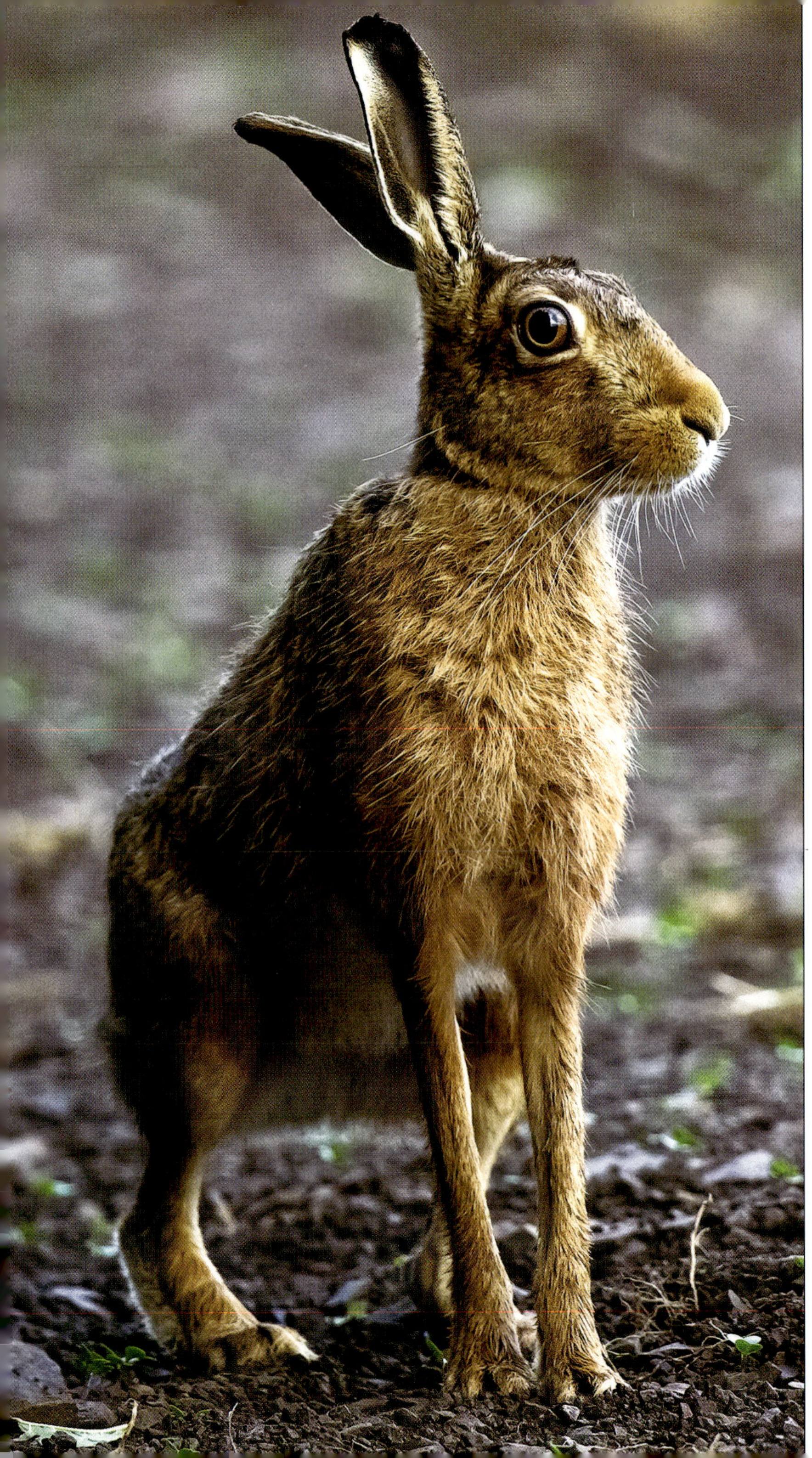

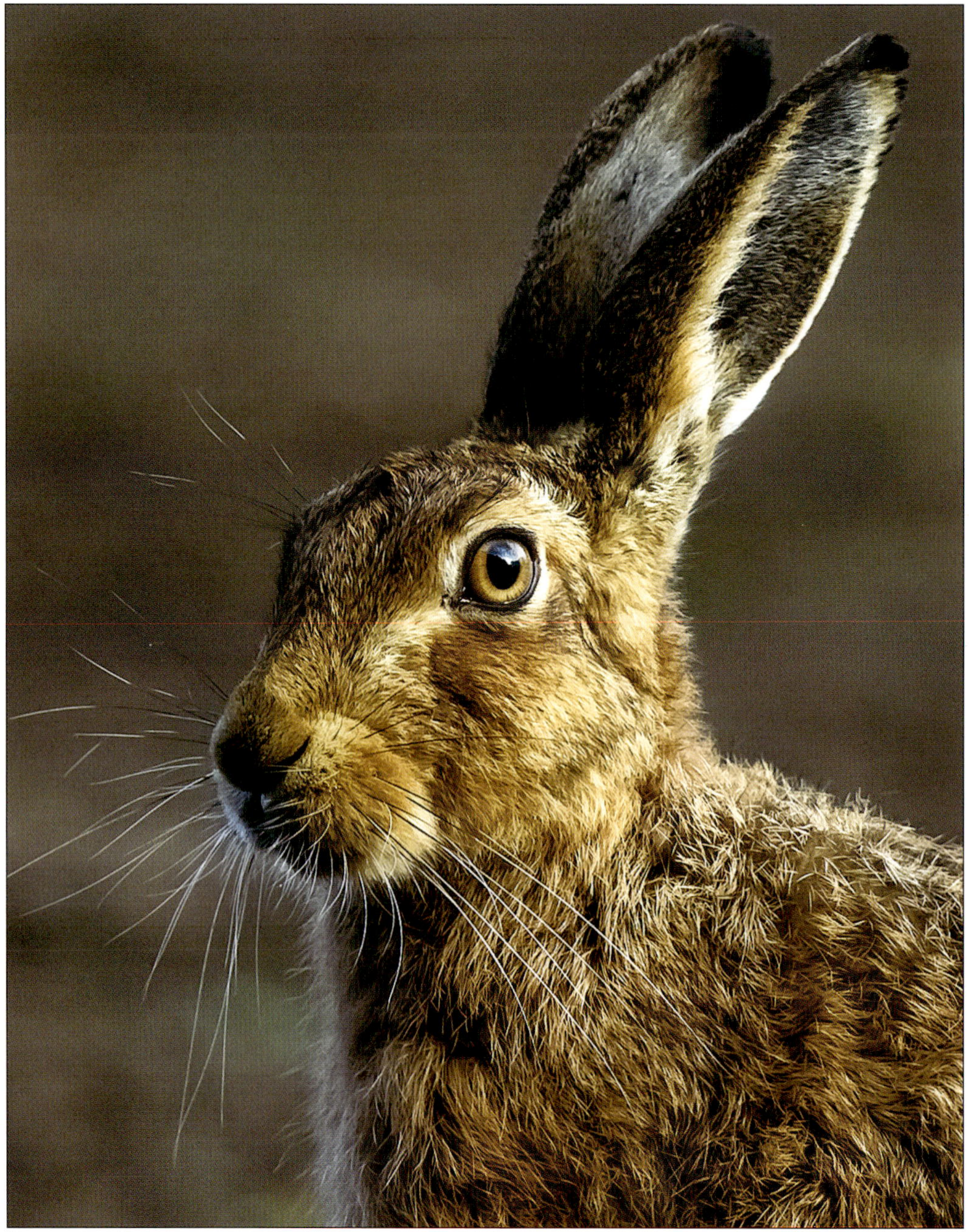

I find a dead pigeon on the road which might make a meal for a buzzard, so ask my farmer friend Steve and Ruth about using their land. The place I have in mind this pre-dawn is a high hill, broad-leaved woods behind, the whole of Corndon and the Long Mynd rearing in front. My hide is a camo-tent, with a fold out seat, and its aim is to turn me into a massive molehill that buzzard will not see. The new day only brings one rather too clever hawk who briefly alights and flies off. However, in this game, you get what you get. And what strolls by, almost within touching distance, are a pair of hares, nibbling on the new field growth for their brekkie.

I appear to be invisible and fire off a couple of shots. Every cat-like whisker sharp, those huge leg muscles compressed to a graceful crouch. Crazy, to put 700mm of lens onto an animal this close. It's electrifying. Hare hears the sound, doesn't know whence it comes, then does what it will habitually do – stands up and stares. It's the perfect pose and my shutter is a happy bunny. Hare's eye is on me, a full-frame moment which I hardly have to crop. My mother used to pick up carnelians on Suffolk beaches and polish them for weeks in her rumbling tumbler. Shining light was revealed when she opened up the box. Here too lie staring jewels, a polished amber of the trees. Then hare's had enough, sprints away into the hedge line. A line from the Rubaiyat of Omar Khayyam runs into my thoughts – *'In Wilderness Is Paradise Now'*.

Hare sitting: Canon 1dx, 500mm + 1.4x, 1/1600 sec, f5.6, ISO 2000
Hare close-up portrait: Canon 1dx, 500mm + 1.4x, 1/1600 sec, f5.6, ISO 1600
Buzzard *Buteo buteo* **flying off:** Canon 7d2, 500mm, 1/3200 sec, f4, ISO 1000

97

There are those not-yet days when I surface from sleep while the sky has still glued all good people to their bed. A sense of promise pulls me from warm covers into a quiet routine of porridge and flasks of hot, sweet Assam, that takes me out the door in a tiptoe to my car, urges me with a middle-aged-crisis-abandon to go hell for leather, not for extreme sports, but soft sunrise. When I reach the hamlet of Asterton, the tiny track that clings to the steep edges of the Mynd awaits me. The stars have cleared off, the light is a pungent blue and I am rewarded. The early mist still bothers the landscape in a pleasing way and that foxglove aches to become my foreground. In the distance, Black Hill and Oakley Mynd are land masses above a shifting sea of sway. My new 16-35 lens proves its stabilized worth and I am able to capture the scene hand-held at 1/60th of a second. I much prefer framing by eye, though will use tripods when light is low. For now, I check every corner of my viewfinder to make sure the picture does what I want it to do…

Even better, as the sun climbs, there is treasure at the side of the road.

The almost ever-shy buzzard, who has a pesky habit of rising from tree in justified annoyance whenever I stop my car, doesn't today. Perhaps that dead branch is too comfy a perch. From inside the car, using the window as temporary tripod, I am staggered by brightness, able to tweak my camera to lovely low ISO and f7.1 to give great sharpness. Here is a portrait of a bird on a branch in the blue.

Dawn from lower slopes of Long Mynd: Canon 6d, 16-35, 1/60 sec, f8, ISO 125 **Buzzard in tree:** Canon 7d2, 500mm, 1/640 sec, f7.1, ISO 100

Common cotton-grass *Eriophorum angustifolium* **&
Devil's Chair with view to Cader Idris:** Canon
1dx, 16-35mm, 1/160 sec, f10, ISO 160
Whitethroat *Sylvia communis* **Brook Vessons,
Stiperstones:** Canon 7d2, 500mm, 1/800 sec, f4,
ISO 200 **Singing linnet** *Carduelis cannabina*,
Stiperstones: Canon 7d2, 500mm, 1/1250 sec, f4,
ISO 200 **Small pearl-bordered fritillary** *Boloria
selene* **Brook Vessons, Stiperstones:** Canon 1dx,
100mm macro, 1/1000 sec, f8, ISO 500

I am hidden on the platform of our tree-house, the copper beech that shades me, my very own jungle camouflage from where I dream of freezing flight and motion. The young swallow is hungry, uses our chapel roof as a table from where it waits for parental deliverance of all good things insectivore. The mother swoops in to feed, delicately dipping her beak into that waiting maw that I catch within 1/3200 of a second. This, the naked eye cannot see, except the blur of it. But technology, despite all its faults, has taken time and compressed it, like coal to diamond in this bright June afternoon.

My friend Wendy Jane has an old family house hidden in the valley just below Corndon Hill – one of the truly remote spots in Shropshire. Each year, the redstarts return, building the nest in the wall a foot from the front door. I go in, on a bright and clear dawn. The hill is quiet, as is the garden surrounding the cottage, a patch of green among the wild vegetation of the hill. I am in luck as the parents are doing what they have to do – nipping round from tree to tree in a caterpillar quest before diving back in to feed their young. During my two hours, I witness a miracle. A sudden flurry of activity and the young are out, taking their first flight! One of them lands on a fence wire and waits patiently to be fed as new lives take off and I have been lucky enough to witness it.

Redstart *Phoenicurus phoenicurus* **mother flying from nest:** Canon 7d2, 500mm, 1/200 sec, f4, ISO 2000 **Redstart mother feeding at nest:** Canon 7d2, 500mm, 1/1250 sec, f4.5, ISO 2500 **Redstart male with grub:** Canon 7d2, 500mm, 1/1000 sec, f4, ISO 1250 **Redstart male feeding fledgling:** Canon 7d2, 500mm, 1/640 sec, f4.5, ISO 1250 **Swallow** *Hirundo rustica* **parent feeding young, Lydbury North:** Canon 7d2, 500mm, 1/3200 sec, f4, ISO 500

Grey Wagtail *Motacilla cinerea*, **Shropshire borders:**
Canon 7d2, 500mm, 1/1250 sec, f4, ISO 2000 **American**
mink *Neovison vison* **swimming in its reflection:** Canon
7d2, 500mm, 1/800 sec, f4.5, ISO 640 **Mink, Clun river,**
Beambridge: Canon 7d2, 500mm, 1/1000 sec, f4.5, ISO 3200

I have been wild-swimming all my life, though back in the 1970's we called it swimming…. It must be my Czech heritage, this love of rivers, lakes, waterfalls and lonely pools. One of my favourite spots is on the river Clun at Beambridge. Over the years, I have found myself staring at the computer screen as the sky beyond the window tempts me out on the ten minute drive, followed by a short walk to a bend in the river I know well. Alder trees still line the bank and the action of winter storms has scooped out perfect deeper hollows to have a summer wallow. On this day, I've exited the water and dried off when I hear a plop behind me. As I turn my head, a sleek form slides into the river. My first thought is otter as I grab my camera, but the body is too dark, the lack of shyness too distinct. I shoot first and ask questions later – even having the delightful feedback from a member of a certain mammal group that posting a mink on their pages is 'inappropriate'. Yes, this is a creature we farmed, then let escape. We are the ones at fault for its place now in the ecosystem. There is a smooth, intelligent, human-like brutality about its efficient nature. Very little (except for otters, who will happily take down a mink) stands in its way. But here it is and it was the first I had ever seen, sharing a dip with me in a little, local river.

The smaller, fluttering inhabitants of Shropshire are well worth chasing. Fine mornings see me hovering over tiny blue butterflies at Prees Heath. Though the season is early, I'm convinced I have captured the Silver-studded blue. It takes some better informed naturalists on Facebook to point out my error, but I still stand by the glory of this snatch of furry sky that is the Common blue. My lens is luckier at Dudmaston woods, where I do find the only site for White admirals in the county, who are in the full throngs of mating, despite the drizzle. And up on Bury Ditches, I search out the rarest of the whites. The Wood white's decline has made it a UK BAP Priority Species candidate. It clings on in only three sites in Shropshire. There is something subtle about its identification – a charcoal smudged underwing. The Gatekeeper and Comma, also taken at Dudmaston, are not particularly uncommon, but one has to admire those scalloped wings and all that plethora of vivid Terry's chocolate orange.

Butterfiies are a species that it is worth ramping up your f-stop for. Increased depth of field can reveal hidden intricacies and whole micro worlds within wing, antennae, abdomen and proboscis. With these pictures, and because these butterflies were quite shy, I used my 500 rather than the macro, or 70-200 to give a compressed and close-up view.

Female White admiral *Limenitis arthemis*, **Dudmaston:** Canon 7d2, 500mm, 1/200 sec, f14, ISO 1000 **Male White admiral, Dudmaston:** Canon 7d2, 500mm, 1/400 sec, f8, ISO 1000
Wood white *Leptidea sinapis*, **Bury Ditches:** Canon 7d2, 500mm, 1/320 sec, f9, ISO 100
Common blue *Polyommatus icarus*, **Prees Heath:** Canon 7d2, 500mm, 1/2000 sec, f8, ISO 500
Comma *Polygonia c-album*, **Dudmaston:** Canon 7d2, 500mm, 1/500 sec, f8, ISO 1000
Gatekeeper *Pyronia tithonus*, **Dudmaston:** Canon 7d2, 500mm, 1/1000 sec, f6.3, ISO 1250

enus Pool near Shrewsbury has become the hangout of choice this year. You never know what you might see, from walking around the site or from one of the hides that look out of over a lake filled with a living landscape of water flurry and activity. Today, attention is drawn by one of the birders to a green movement in the green of the lake bank. I am assaulted by colour – a vivid red stripe, and a back easily as shiny as a hummingbird. It's a male, possibly a young one, as indicated by the touch of red in the moustachial stripe. As for that eye, well eyes are what it's all about today – from the statuesque stare of the green woodpecker hidden among the summer vegetation, to the male kingfisher with a meal that requires some acrobatic tossing. My fast shutter speed is a great enabler, showing the button eye of the kingfisher and the rather forlorn and ghostly eye of the stickleback before it is swallowed in a single gulp.

Green woodpecker *Picus viridis*, **Venus Pool:** Canon 1dx, 500mm + 2x, 1/1600 sec, f8, ISO 400 **Kingfisher** *Alcedo atthis* **flying off perch:** Canon 7d2, 500mm + 1.4x, 1/2500 sec, f6.3, ISO 800 **Kingfisher juggling Three-spined stickleback** *Gasterosteus aculeatus***:** Canon 7d2, 500mm + 1.4x, 1/2500 sec, f6.3, ISO 1250

Thus like the sad presaging Raven that tolls
The sicke mans passeport in her hollow beake,
And in the shadow of the silent night
Doth shake contagion from her sable wings

The Jew of Malta Act 2: Scene 1 (Marlowe)

Marlowe got it wrong,
    and though you're known as goddess
      of the caves,
Odin's spy to whisper all the world
    its woe into his ear,
      Corbie Craw, you mean much more to me:

For when my own car was a cave
    and you were stately in your fly by past,
I caught that momentary sheen,
    was made blind by your magnificence.

If you've evolved to be the night by chance
    if such genetic pull is all there is,
Then I refute and hold you to the dawn,
    to the Mynd, where heather lies in bloom,
A purple susurrus of rainbow cut
    and fallen to a summer month.

There now, claws out,
    curlicue of sky, you flare and feather wing
To brake, to slow, to clutch again
    at land and gravity
Omen not of earth's grave muck
    but hammer of the bright dawn's luck.

Raven *Corvus corax* **at dawn, Long Mynd:**
Canon 7d2, 500mm, 1/1600 sec, f4.5, ISO 320
Raven landing in the heather: Canon 7d2,
500mm, 1/1600 sec, f4.5, ISO 320

Dark Skies

How can we lift the stars from
    their influence,
      summon their crazy-eyed stare
and make them bow before
    our inconsiderate justice?

What weighs heavily in their favour?
They are but pattern and gravity,
    darkness ground beneath their
    mercurial, unshod feet.

Feel no pity, as they loose away from us,
    over a span that only
imagination and mathematics
    can comprehend.

But for now, lie on this rock with me,
    this quartzite patch where
    our own pitiful
illumination cannot reach.

This is day extinguished,
    the candle of our smallness put out
as all around us, the vast
    and heaving deeps sigh
across the echo of a lighted sky.

Milky Way over the Nipstone: Canon 6d, Samyang 14mm, 25 sec, f2.8 ISO 3200
Peregrine falcon *Falco peregrinus* **in flight, Long Mynd:** Canon 7d2, 500mm, 1/2500 sec, f7.1, ISO 800 **Hobby** *Falco subbuteo* **in flight, Long Mynd:** Canon 1dx, 500mm + 1.4x, 1/2500 sec, f5.6, ISO 500

The Mynd is filled with hawking and hunting this summer. To see hobby stoop and zip over the smoothed out, treeless landscape is an honour, and to catch the colouring of peregrine, the wonderful underwing patterning up close while trying to hold the heavy 500 lens in my hand brings a perfect morning to a happy close. The art of photographing birds in motion through sky is not to believe what your camera wants to do, which is expose for the light behind the bird. This is the reason, many bird in flight shots, taken on Auto settings, end up showing no more than dark silhouettes. But if you read the light, overexpose by up to two stops so that the camera reads the light from the falcon, not the sky, you are in with a chance of gaining all that colour. Then it's a matter of good focus and tracking skills, which is where the technique of back-button focusing comes in handy, separating out the shutter butter from the AF button and enabling closer control. Then its practice, practice, practice. There are no short cuts for framing creatures moving at speed through their own element with ease.

Female Red grouse *Lagopus lagopus scotica* **in the heather at dawn, Long Mynd:** Canon 7d2, 500mm, 1/1600 sec, f6.3, ISO 640 **Flying grouse in a misty dawn, Long Mynd:** Canon 1dx, 70-200mm, 1/2000 sec, f2.8, ISO 1600 **Meadow pipit** *Anthus pratensis* **at dawn, Long Mynd:** Canon 7d2, 500mm, 1/1250 sec, f4.5, ISO 250 **Male red grouse at dusk, Long Mynd:** Canon 7d2, 500mm, 1/100 sec, f4.5, ISO 8000

I cannot keep away from this luminescent heather, as if the uplands are filled with purple fireflies. Dawn turns the carpet iridescent, a female grouse almost lost amongst the flowering except for a beady eye. Even the mist cannot keep me away, hiding three grouse who flare up among the sheep. The meadow pipit is common enough up here to be called the trash bird of heathland, the opposite is sadly true. As with so many species, the decline since the 1950s has been dramatic and sees this pretty insect feeder on the Amber list for conservation concern. One night, at the end of August, stalking a sighting of hen harrier at Pole Cottage right on top of the Mynd, I meet my fellow naturalist Dave. It is he, with far more years experience, and now in the beyond dusk near-dark, who spies a male red grouse flying to roost. I stalk towards the bird, not even sure my canon 7d2 can focus. At 8000 ISO, the bird stares back at me, sharp among the colour, lifted from the gloom. Moments like these I live for.

There is wildlife and there is wild light, a shy, mercurial creature, best seen once a month. The spotting scope I use is an app called *The Photographer's Ephemeris*, which understands orbit and gravity, she who tugs at tidal strings and who I dream of, rising over the sharp etched edge of solid scree we call the Stiperstones. I have come up here four months in a row, walking with the heavy tripod and even heavier long lens that I will need to complete my task. But every month, as dusk comes on and the sky behind is slowly taking out the day, she has eluded me, using the usual excuse of cloud banks and mist. But I am persistent in a vision that search engines tell me does not yet exist. I plant my three-legged stand, and hope that 400mm of telephoto will do this shy one justice. The app has told me where to be and where she will arise. I wait, get cold, grab the incredible sunset, glorious with heather below and tint above until I sense the spreading of a brightness by the rocks and almost cannot breathe. The moon! The moon! I say, to myself for I am alone, except for her, who is hunted but not afraid, who turns the heather to a darker, heavy purple and the sky a pungent blue. A week later, my first ever photo is published in the Guardian, but it is she who must take credit as the full moon rose over the Devil's Chair on the Stiperstones one perfect August night.

Stiperstones sunset: Canon 6d, 100-400mm mk2, 1/30 sec, f9, ISO 200, tripod **Full moon over the Devil's Chair:** Canon 6d, 100-400mm mk2 at 400mm, 1/6 sec, f9, ISO 500, tripod, single exposure developed from raw

Bury Ditches at dawn: Canon 6d, 16-35mm, 1/125 sec, f8, ISO 50
Stiperstones sunset: Canon 6d, 17-40mm, 1/20 sec, f8, ISO 400, grad filters

Southern Hawker larval exo-skeleton: Canon 6d, 100mm macro, 1/1000 sec, f6.3, ISO 800 **White-faced darter** *Leuchorrhinia dubia*, **Whixall Moss:** Canon 7d2, 500mm, 1/640 sec, f8, ISO 320 **Four-spotted chaser** *Libellula quadrimaculata*, **Whixall Moss:** Canon 7d2, 500mm, 1/500 sec, f10, ISO 640 **Southern hawker** *Aeshna cyanea*, **Beambridge:** Canon 650d, 55-250mm, 1/640 sec, f8, ISO 400

Flight and focus. The human eye can see so much, but really so little. Perhaps we should regard our cameras as aids. They sometimes add to sight, by taking time and slicing it to a smallness that might reveal a miracle. The dragonfly when still is quite a catch, for sure. But when they are on the move, the trick is to understand how they use the air to create predictable patterns. They have their favourite routes and if you can anticipate and find a moment where they hover briefly, brief being the word, you are in with a chance. This year, during a workshop with the wonderful Mark Sisson, I peered closer at the waving reeds around Walcot Lake, finding the exo-skeloton of a Southern hawker dragonfly. I've found the common four-spotted chaser and the rare white-faced darter at the bog pools of Whixall Moss, the male emperor dragonfly at Pantglas and the southern hawker at Aston-on-Clun. They have carried the whole season in their chasing, darting, hawking souls, appearing in May and still buzzing about at the end of September.

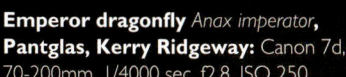

Emperor dragonfly *Anax imperator*,
Pantglas, Kerry Ridgeway: Canon 7d,
70-200mm, 1/4000 sec, f2.8, ISO 250

Sparrows on hedge, Bury Ditches: Canon
1dx, 500mm + 1.4x, 1/2000 sec, f5.6, ISO 2000
Ducks and geese at Clunbury: Canon 7d2,
100-400mk2, 1/160 sec, f5.6, ISO 500

September is still hot enough for me to swim the high reaches of the Clun at Clunbury. But the water holds a secret. Its sudden chill carries the promise of the months ahead. Four years ago, I came to this spot for a swim. Depression already had me in its clutches. A few days later I was in hospital and extremely ill. But, like the flowing of this river, all my sickness did was scour out the old and bring in the new. My old career also went downstream and was replaced with this. On that day, shivering with more than premonition, I was clambering out of the water when I heard a splash. A large shape slipped from the Clun's clutch and I knew it was not dog, or goose, but otter, sharing a dip with me, harbinger of hope for all the change to come, despite the dark days that lay ahead. Back then, my illness took me through months of despair for me and my family. Now, my healing takes place right here, in the outdoors, acting as a reflector for the unexpected moments that pass before my eyes. How can anyone be unhappy, when the very ethos of nature is harmony out of dreaming chaos?

Autumn

Grey squirrel *Sciurus carolinensis* **gathering acorns:** Canon 7d2, 500mm, 1/160 sec, f4.5, ISO 400
Red kite *Milvus milvus* **in flight:** Mears Barn, Canon 1dx, 500mm + 1.4x, 1/2000 sec, ISO 1600
Morning mist, Lydbury North: Canon 650d, 100-400L, 1/800 sec, f7.1 ISO 400

I love autumn. The dying of colour that marks the end of summer goes into a strange reversal, as if the trees are dreaming what it is like to flower. Leaves become creatures in their own right, with chameleon qualities and the ability to crinkle and curl like ageing gymnasts. We have a September, warm enough to keep up my dips into one of the hidden pools of Walcot, wallowing in water as the last dragonflies sing their zipped up harmonies.

I don't need to search far for wilderness and find evidence in the most unlikely spots. Where the river Severn loops through Shrewsbury, I have spent most of the year jealous of frequent otter sightings near English Bridge. Whenever I make the drive, and spend hours patrolling the bridge and the parks on either side, my only reward is the odd sun-fanning cormorant or a display of endless gull-tactics that does not take my breath away. But this season, sprinkled with patience and persistence, gives me the treasure of a fishing dog-otter who lives up Rae brook, who now comes out into the sunshine.

On the Stiperstones, we come across a juvenile cuckoo who has not yet learned human fear. To crawl this close and catch caterpillar-eating behaviour is exciting, especially as the bird is unusually late to still be here. I hope it managed to make the journey to Africa.

Early autumn has other surprises up her sleeve. Instead of billowing handkerchiefs, or doves, the temperature change brings the magical apparition of mist that is not above and around, but below. Climb a hill at dawn or dusk and you might catch what the Met Office calls 'valley fog'. Tiny water droplets suspended in the air are stuck in the valleys because warmer air is passing up above. Science aside, to see the whole land swaddled, to drive up into the high places, out of hand's breadth visibility into clear light, is a miracle of weather. Add in skies that pass as full on, commercial orangeries, and it looks like I have gone mad with my saturation slider. Such colour appears surreal and artificial. It isn't.

For the first time, I have been witness to two of the great spectacles particular to this season. Many people have seen incredible pictures of salmon leaping in Scotland and Alaska. We have our own story I have been able to follow in the Severn and the Teme. It's a tale of bravery, of muscles, of that which is of water, briefly becoming airborne. It's also a slow deepening of a technique that can frame in perfect clarity, that moment when a salmon, intent on upstream spawn, flicks from the surface and announces its relationship to sky. I am in awe.

I am fortunate enough to be taken in by the forestry ranger to one of the secret deer-rutting stands in Mortimer forest near Ludlow. Over several visits, I witness fallow bucks and a long-haired buck, a sub-species that exists only in this wood and nowhere else in the world.

Light and colour. Last blooms and dancing hares. Trees, blown of all their worldly goods, and at last, an intervention. In my garden, feeders are hung on pretty, foraged sticks. Flash is applied to freeze motion, show that even the commonest garden bird is a little fling of wonder which my supply of nuts might help to keep alive in the cold and coming months.

Female Red grouse *Lagopus lagopus*
in heather *Calluna vulgaris***, Long Mynd:**
Canon 7d2, 500mm, 1/400 sec, f4.5,
ISO 125 **Mute swan** *Cygnus olor* **at**
dusk, Walcot Lake: Canon 650d,
100-400L, 1/160 sec, f5.6 ISO 800

This is my second bout of otterly good fortune this year. It appears to follow the pattern of the first. Many fruitless visits, hanging out with other photo geeks, alert for any trail of bubbles under the water. For the first of October, the weather is t-shirtable – the outdoors becomes my office – and leaning against the balustrade, looking upstream from the weir is a good place to spend the working day. Apart from the odd Goosander, the morning passes uneventfully with my good friends Ric and Stuart from the Shropshire Wildlife Trust. A few locals stop and tell us about their sightings and I am convinced the Shrewsbury otters will never grace my presence. After a serious coffee and sarnie from Ginger and Co, I'm ready to head back out on watch.

Otters are creatures of habit, but this dog-otter, when he turns up, doesn't care for pattern. His only interest is decent fishy bite in what must be a productive river. I cannot believe buses, cars and pedestrians are going past, about their afternoon business, while I chase a wonderful sleekness through bank and bushes, straining muscles as I hold my heavy telephoto. Yes, it is said, they are on every Shropshire river now, but there is something about a large, wild mammal doing his town centre thing that is both heartening and hopeful.

Dog Otter, English Bridge: Canon 7d2, 500mm, 1/1000 sec, f4.5, ISO 500 **Dog otter shaking head, English Bridge:** Canon 7d2, 500mm + 1.4x, 1/1000 sec, f6.3, ISO 1250 **Dog otter staring portrait, English Bridge:** Canon 7d2, 500mm + 1.4x, 1/1000 sec, f5.6, ISO 1000 **Female Goosander** *Mergus mergansa*, **English Bridge, Shrewsbury:** Canon 7d2, 500mm, 1/160 sec, f7.1, ISO 100

We have raised our family in a little village, and somehow settled further in as twenty years passed us by. I feel part of the flora and fauna furniture. On misty October mornings, the view from Oakley Mynd, down to our village, is a wonder. On nearby Linley Hill, one of the old beech trees long ago blown over by winter winds, now gives new life to porcelain fungus. Even better, as I work with some fill flash to light the underside of the fungi, I notice on the resulting picture that I have also caught the far moon.

We have pheasants at the top of our lane, bred from a local estate. I wouldn't normally be interested in photographing them, but this bird on a bale in perfect morning sun presented an opportunity. Especially as, when I focused, it went beautifully bonkers, dancing about and kicking up the hay. Was this a form of male braggadachio? Possibly. However, this is the reason I spend hours, days, months walking field and forest. Eventually, something interesting is bound to happen. When I put the pic on facebook, a press agency contacted me and a few days later, my Mears Barn pheasant was on page four of the Times. I made sure to give a copy to my farmer friends Ruth and Steve.

Mist over Lydbury North at dawn:
Canon 6d, 16-35mm, 1/80 sec, f16, ISO 125
Displaying pheasant *Phasianus colchicus*
Mears Barn: Canon 7d2, 500mm, 1/2000 sec, f4, ISO 320
Porcelain fungus *Oudemansiella mucida*
Linley Beeches: Canon 7d2, 16-35mm, 1/250 sec, f16, ISO 400, fill flash

Another morning out with Simon, the Stiperstones ranger. We had hopes of birds on berries, but the redwings and fieldfares have already stripped the bushes bare. The Land Rover chugs over the tiny paths, disturbing a few grouse who cackle off into the browning heather. There is a greyness to the day which slowly seeps into my mood. Never give up hope. On our last traverse, as we dip down beneath the Devil's chair, Simon pulls the car to a halt. On the track is what looks like a young sparrowhawk. As ever, it flies off. We have a decision. Do we kit up and head into the heather, or do we accept our mission is pretty much pointless? Instinct kicks in. Upland, and the heather that coats it, is a bouncy, hard to negotiate terrain. No matter how high your boots, stuff gets in. I know it's not jungle but the going is slow. Luckily for us, there are endless, worn grouse paths that enable us to climb towards where the bird went. Thirty yards later, and creeping slowly, we are greeted with a sight that takes a dull day and gilds it with all the gold leaf of an icon. 'It's a juvenile cuckoo!' the normally unflappable Simon whispers, as he trains his binoculars. Time to do my job. I have a sinking feeling that the cuckoo, which is probably a female from the coloured wing markings, will no doubt fly off before I get a single shot.

      She doesn't. Instead, we spend a good half an hour, crouching and wriggling on bellies to close in on her very relaxed behaviour – a very vigorous bout of late-caterpillar munching, followed by a relax and even a snooze. Late is the word, as although the juveniles often migrate later than the adults, 8th of October is very tardy indeed. This was not the only sighting of this wonderful bird and I wish her well, particularly as numbers have dropped by 65% in recent years.

Juvenile Cuckoo *Cuculus canorus* **with caterpillar, Stiperstones:** Canon 7d2, 500mm, 1/1250 sec, f4, ISO 1000 **Juvenile cuckoo sleeping, Stiperstones:** Canon 7d2, 500mm, 1/1600 sec, f4.5, ISO 800 **Juvenile cuckoo in flight, Stiperstones:** Canon 7d2, 500mm, 1/1600 sec, f4, ISO 1000

I have lived in Shropshire all my adult life, but only just discovered the delights of Mortimer Forest near Ludlow. A new friend, Ian Slater, meets me before dawn in Vinalls car park to see if we can find some deer. We can't, but the sunrise over far Clee hill and incredible morning that follows are good consolation prizes. I also bump into the Marches Forest wildlife ranger Alan Reid, who takes me into an active rutting spot. This involves a drive along one of the many forestry tracks, and then the old favourite of mine, belly-wriggling through dense conifers. The wind is blowing towards us, so we are in with a chance. Chance turns to blessing as a single-antlered fallow buck stands right between the trees only twenty yards away. Later, Alan takes me back to the same site but from the other side, where a glade looks particularly promising. It takes two visits before I work up my invisibility skills sufficiently to frame these gloriously wild creatures. One of the young bucks is entirely unaware of my presence and goes to sleep. With those hair-tufts, top-knot and a hirsute underbelly, Alan assures me later that this is the unique long-haired fallow, a sub-species of fallow deer, that thrives in this wood and nowhere else in the world. Discovered in the 1950s by Forestry Ranger Gerald Springthorpe, this is a Shropshire wonder to witness. It also turns out that the older buck with magnificent antlers is about 10% long-hair, evidenced by ear tufts and top-knot.

View of Clee Hill from Mortimer Forest, Jack Hill, at dawn: Canon 6d, 50mm 1.4, 1/80 sec, f2.8, ISO 640 **Morning sunshine, Mortimer Forest:** Canon 6d, 16-35mm, 1/250 sec, f18, ISO 400 **Fallow buck** *Dama dama* **with single antler, Mortimer Forest:** Canon 7d2, 70-200mm, 1/15 sec, f3.2, ISO 10000

Stalking

I have read the wind this morning,
south by southwest,
whereby a hopeful chapter hangs.
I walk the Elan Valley pipeline,
under a broadleaf highway
filled with the yellowing of autumn.
Beneath me water from high Welsh fastness
thrums to Brum
helped by the hand of gravity.
 Far from the cry of walked dogs,
 I hear the rough, reverberating phlegm of the forest.
Andrew, go dark. Hat, gloves, the covering up of human,
every silent step a move in fieldcraft chess.
 Leave the track,
 Climb and crawl, slow,
 To a glade where only half the day gets through,
 Conifers now my friends,
 Every frond a camouflage
It works. For in that light a
young buck strolls, a stream of hair
pouring from his ears.
Chilled to the point of sitting. Then sleep.
 I frame him with a shutter set to soundless.
 Though my heart strains to a marathon,
 He does not know me.
The bellowing begins again, is enough
for the young punk to leave the scene, admit
he's lower down the rung.
 Now, I beg of you, come from the darkness of wood,
 Bring yourself; the points on your antlers, a constellation.
I see you through fern, wilting of bracken, deep spindled thicket,
power in those brindled haunches.
The darkly glass, poured into the moment
we meet in the middle of the rut.
 I am no longer evergreen, nor lost in the shadows,
 Buck rises, meets my eye, slow, then fast
 Sprint and melt;
He's gone, muscle made to leap into the barky dusk
leaving behind the scent of sweet musk.

All in Mortimer Forest: Sleeping long-haired buck *Dama dama***:** Canon 7d2, 100-400L, 1/200 sec, f5.6, ISO 800   **Long-haired buck standing:** Canon 7d2, 100-400L, 1/250 sec, f5.6, ISO 2500   **Fallow buck sitting:** Canon 7d2, 100-400L, 1/320 sec, f5.6, ISO 4000   **Fallow buck antlers:** Canon 7d2, 100-400L, 1/320 sec, f5, ISO 2500

How could I know there was another country only miles from here? The whole of Shropshire is drowned in a thick-fogged seeping away of light, as if the sun has been banished like Cordelia, for simply being too warm and loving. My friend Caitlin rings up, offering the lure of starlings in the fields behind her house. She lives on Long Mountain, an apt description of a lifted landscape that hovers above the porous edges of Shropshire. One minute, I am driving up a single winding spindle of a road with headlights on in second gear, unable even to see the next bend. The next, miles of mist are behind and below and the weather is a glorious echo of old seasons. The blue sky appears quite impossible and I smile as I drive along the uplands to Caitlin's sunny abode. A welcome cup of sweet tea is plonked in my hand as we watch the first starlings come in. Perhaps not quite a murmuration, more a sibilant whisper. There is a sound that accompanies such numbers in flight – a quiet hiss as I marvel at this carpet of feather and intention lifting above the ploughed earth. We spend the next hour chasing fog, trying to find the best shot, which turns out to be actually in the field right behind her house, where the mist has turned the distant Welsh hills into islands. Who knows where the gate in the field leads? If I were carrying a little coracle for such calm turbulence, I might put it out just behind those woods. My paddle would sink into a different sea, where I could make my way at last to the west, to peace, to freedom from all anxiety. As Edward Thomas said 'some day I shall think this a happy day.'

Starling *Sturnus vulgaris* **murmuration, Long Mountain:**
Canon 1dx, 24-70mm, 1/400 sec,f4, ISO 400 **Sunset with mist,
Long Mountain:** Canon 1dx, 24-70mm, 1/80 sec,f8, ISO 160
(previous pages) **Sunset and mist above New Invention:**
Canon 1dx, 24-70mm, 1/50 sec,f2.8, ISO 3200

As my photography develops, there are quite often pictures lurking in the river of my mind before I take them. Like dreams, they rarely leap into reality, but once in a while, with work, technique, weather, grace, good fortune and understanding of light, the shots come together. Salmon are both tricky and awesome. They jump so fast and unpredictably, it's hard to focus. With a wide angle lens, pre-focusing a third of the way into a shot and setting depth of field to f8 and beyond, the first hurdle can be covered. Light is the next challenge. A dark fish against water. What to do? Three flash speedlites cover this angle, a fashion shoot for a fish. How to freeze motion? HSS or high-speed-sync set to 1/1000 of a second. Not particularly fast, but the flash does all the work. Then make sure your exposure doesn't lose the background – which needs a camera happy with high ISO, preferably full frame, and a very fast shutter speed, which my Canon 1dx is perfect for. A rock solid tripod, a trigger release and watch the water for that incredible moment. All this, in the centre of Shrewsbury and a little weir on the river Teme south of Ludlow, not Scotland or Alaska!

Dawn over Shrewsbury weir, river Severn: Canon 1dx, 16-35mm, 1/2 sec , f11, ISO 160, tripod **Photo of Andrew in River Teme, Ludlow:** taken by Richard Shucksmith on iphone 4s, 4.12mm, 1/120 sec, f2.4, ISO 80 **Leaping Salmon** *Salmo salar* **close-up portrait:** Canon 1dx, 16-35mm, 1/1250 sec, f10, ISO 640, tripod, remote cable, 4 remote Canon 600 rx-et flashes

Cock and hen salmon leaping: Canon 1dx, 16-35mm, 1/1250 sec, f8, ISO 1250, tripod, remote cable, 4 remote Canon 600 rx-et flashes **Single salmon leaping with far sunlight:** Canon 1dx, 16-35mm, 1/1250 sec, f13, ISO 800, tripod, remote cable, 4 remote Canon 600 rx-et flashes **Salmon leaping at Ashford Carbonel, Ludlow:** Canon 1dx, 16-35mm, 1/1600 sec, f8, ISO 2000, tripod, remote cable, 3 remote Canon 600 rx-et flashes

Flight

Begun in a redd with her tail as a spade
    To push away gravel for eggs to be laid
The male so tired as he spills his seed
    Making new life in a current of need
Alevin, fry, parr and spring smolt
    The river behind now, with surf to vault
Out in the deeps to feed up and grow
    Until one season returning to sow
How they remember, what is their spell
    Some say is simply a sense of smell
As they enter a mouth they knew long ago
    No food in this river, they fight the far flow
Here in the heartlands, high in the Teme
    We stare at a weir, and hold to their dream
For these are their mountains, silver to scale
    Over and over, we cry as they fail
In wonder of faith, their efforts forgive
    A death in this river, and yet they will live

Salmo Salar, returns from the deep,
    The language of Latin: Salire ... 'to leap'

The land is hushed today, a thick mist that lays like quiet over the valley. High on the Long Mynd, my car is reduced to a crawling sloth, as I can't see even a few yards ahead. I am absurdly optimistic as I head along the old portway, that once carried Neolithic traders safely above the boggy woodlands below. Surely something must be out and about today? I am relying on the fact that grouse not only like heather but also a serving of road grit. As heather is tough and fibrous, ingesting grit helps them to break down their main foodstuff. I hear a familiar cackle just off the road to my right. Once again, my car has rendered me semi-invisible. I catch the male as he calls before striding off into the misty morning.

Male Red grouse calling in mist, Long Mynd: Canon 7d2, 500mm, 1/500 sec, f4.5, ISO 1000
Buzzard *Buteo buteo* **on post at sunset, Rhos Fiddle, Clun:** Canon 7d2, 500mm, 1/800 sec, f4, ISO 200

The dipper's dense plumage is great protection from the icy water it spends much time in. Its feathers gain their wonderful sheen from the waterproof oil produced in large quantities in its preen gland. Strong wings are not so much for flight, as flight through fast-flowing water as it turns over pebbles to see what it can find. On this wet, cold afternoon, with a lack of salmon at Ludford weir, in Ludlow, this little bird was about its feeding business, unbothered by a guy using a railing as an improvised tripod. What struck me above all though, was the moment it paused to rest on a rock, and revealed the true magic of the dipper – a white, feathered eyelid. Did the dipper know its own beauty, that here in a combo of cream and brown was our very own vintage autumn?

Dipper *Cinclus cinclus* **with food, Ludford Weir, Ludlow:** Canon 7d2, 500mm, 1/640 sec, f4.5, ISO 2000
Dipper dipping, Ludford Weir, Ludlow: Canon 7d2, 500mm, 1/1000 sec, f4, ISO 2000 **Dipper portrait with white eyelid, Ludford Weir, Ludlow:** Canon 7d2, 500mm, 1/60 sec, f4, ISO 160

View from Brown Clee: Canon 6d, 16-35mm, 1/160 sec, f13, ISO 320, handheld
Fungi in woods near Edgton: Canon 6d, 16-35mm, 1/100 sec, f4, ISO 500, handheld

Wilderland

Crows are conjuring the dusk.

    The moon's a bitten bit of rusk.

Buzzard sings her mewing cry,

    Prowling, feathered cat-of-sky,

And there among the winter beet

    I'm given grace, a priceless treat

For tired, telescopic eyes:

    Two hares, and then to my surprise

Like a midnight striking hand,

    Male and female, upright stand

Then push out paws, begin to fight,

    A furry flash of grey and white.

Such a bold and brave display

    As on hind legs they swerve and sway,

Ears stuck up like lollipops,

    I breathe too loud, the battle stops.

They turn to statues cut from bark.

    I blink. They sprint into the dark,

Leaving me to simply stare

    At a dream no longer there.

Oh what delights this world unlocks

    To let me see two hares that box.

Male and female Brown hare *Lepus europeaus* **boxing:** Canon 7d2, 500mm, 1/400 sec, f4, ISO 100 **Male and female hare running:** Canon 7d2, 500mm, 1/400 sec, f4, ISO 100 **Hare preening:** Canon 7d2, 500mm, 1/1250 sec, f4, ISO 400 **Hare grazing:** Canon 7d2, 500mm, 1/1250 sec, f4, ISO 500

Female Blackbird *Turdus merula* **in Spindleberry**
*Euonymus europaeus***:** Canon 7d2, 500mm, 1/1250 sec, f4.5,
ISO 800 **Feral ponies** *Equus ferus* **in the mist, Long**
Mynd: Canon 6d, 16-35mm, 1/200 sec, f8, ISO500

**Sunrise over Lydbury North with frozen Parasol
mushroom** *Macrolepiota procera***:** Canon 6d, 16-35mm, 0.8 sec, f14,
ISO 125, tripod, focus stacked shot. **Blakeridge Woods, Cefn
Einion:** Canon 6d, 100-400L, 1/250 sec, f9, ISO 1000

I have moved my photographic work indoors, into the kitchen, to be precise. I have my camera, tripod, and remote release cable. This is not advanced food photography, though the process is food related. The great British habit of feeding garden birds in winter has actually reversed the decline in several species. What I am about today, is to reflect the miraculous in the everyday. The remote flashes, arrayed just out of sight, have the special power of stalling motion, of catching and transfixing movement that mortal eyes could never see. The flared wing of a robin turns our common visitor into a rare flamenco dancer. The common blue-tit becomes a vibrant stealth bomber. All these birds must eat for the cold winter ahead. The urge of life, even at this crux of the year is insistent and vital, as the world turns and I in my turn, enjoy this short, culinary hibernation from within the warmth of home and hearth.

Robin *Erithacus rubecula* **with flared wing:**
Canon 1dx, 500mm +1.4x, 1/4000 sec, f5.6, ISO 1600, tripod, 3 Yongnuo flashes on remote.
Blue tit *Cyanistes caeruleus*, **Lydbury North:**
Canon 1dx, 500mm +1.4x, 1/4000 sec, f5.6, ISO 1600, tripod, 3 Yongnuo flashes on remote.

Index of photographs